HOW TO WRITE A FANTASY BOOK DESCRIPTION

A Step-by-Step System for Writing Blurbs That Sell

JESPER SCHMIDT

CONTENTS

WRITING THE BOOK DESCRIPTION

EDITING THE BOOK DESCRIPTION

FEEDBACK AND FORMATTING

BONUS

APPENDICES

IS THIS BOOK FOR ME?

F rom time to time, I post this picture of Gollum, from J.R.R. Tolkien's legendarium, on Twitter:

"We have to write the blurb, but we hates it"

… And every single time, without fault, it triggers an avalanche of reactions and responses.

Why?

Because the thought of condensing our beautiful, and carefully constructed, fantasy novel of 100,000 words down to only a few hundred is angst-provoking. In a way, we would probably have a lot in common with a painter. Had he been handed three colors and told to create a masterpiece, it would make him break out in sweat as much as going to the dentist with an infected root canal.

Sounds familiar?

Yes. That's because we are fantasy writers – words are like magic spells to us. We don't want them mistreated and used to write book descriptions that read like ad copy.

Whether we like it or not, though, book descriptions *are* a crucial factor when a reader decides to buy your book or just ignore it. Having great confidence in the quality of your books isn't enough. It won't guide the reader to *wanting* the book.

Granted: ebooks are cheap. Yet, we still need to make the reader *want* it more than keeping that five-dollar bill in their pocket. To make a living from writing, we *have to* sell books. Heck, even our very nature is working against us.

We human beings tend to avoid what makes us feel uncomfortable and, as a result, we end up putting in a substandard effort when it comes to producing strong book descriptions.

My first blurb was awful – more about that a little later – but the best part about writing is that it's like a muscle. It grows with time and in conjunction with the amount of effort you put into exercising it. The art of blurb-writing can be improved by practice.

Hidden within these pages is a step-by-step system that is as painless and professional as it is effective. It matters not if you are self-published or attempting to write a book descriptions that will catch the attention of agents and publishers. By following the path laid out in this book, any writer can learn how to conceive appealing blurbs and captivating tag lines.

My goal is for you to come away enlightened and with strong skill that will boost your career as a fiction author.

And one more thing: This book doesn't contain guidance on how to write a synopsis (the 1-2 page short form requested by publishers) or an agent query letter (the letter you draft to attract a literary agent). However, at the point of writing, this is the only book on the market that solely focuses on fantasy. All the other books, and there are some great ones among them, are approaching the subject from a broader perspective.

The teachings from here on in will be jam-packed with tips and tricks which are easy-to-understand and to do.

Why give your best to produce an incredible rich and wonderful tale, only to spend a minute or two writing its description?

IT'S TIME

W elcome, dear fantasy author and colleague.

I'm absolutely thrilled that you have allowed me to be your guide into the world of fantasy book descriptions. Thank you.

Now, the first stop on this journey will be focusing on the reader. There are some important things to get across in coming chapters before we get to the juicy parts on how to write incredible book descriptions.

If there is anything I have learned from writing tons of proposals in my corporate life, it is how to cut to the chase. While an offer to a client is not the same as a book description, the underlying mindset is very similar. You need to acquire competencies if you are to deliver a message concisely and clearly.

To that end, I have to mention how I love fact-based information – it just works well together with my analytical way of thinking.

So, this became the approach I took. I put in the effort and began to transform my aforementioned business skills into developing book descriptions that would sell. I knew I had to learn. I knew it could be learned.

I read a ton of non-fiction on writing blurbs. I researched the bestselling fantasy books. I analyzed the classics. I took all that I learned and coupled it with my in-depth knowledge of writing effective copy and proposals.

My blurbs needed to sound more like this:

**"Welcome to the Magical Death Match.
For five long years, I've wanted just one thing – to find my
sister Rowan. Her disappearance tore a hole in my life."**

*"Attack by Magic" by Linsey Hall
– Amazon Best Sellers Rank: #85 Paid in Kindle Store*

Pow! That's more like it.

By the way, being in the top 100 on the Kindle Store speaks volumes, so it's worth paying attention.

In full transparency, though, there is more to the above-mentioned blurb, but I focused on the first two lines to help paint a picture of how readers are looking for books. They will look at cover art, check the title and price, perhaps even the star rating, and they will read the description.

If we have got them this far, this is now the *most* critical point in the readers' decision-making process. This is where our blurb needs to come flying into the ring like the professional boxer, Muhammad Ali. It needs to pack enough punch to end the fight early. If we get into fifteen rounds we will lose.

In other words, it's all about instantly delivering intrigue and hooking the reader. Within seconds, the decision to read the story or not is taken. The "back button" is constantly tempting the

5

reader to click it and browse for something else. That's where the sale is lost, and with it, a potentially long-time reader.

Attention-grabbing blurbs, with a "hook" compelling enough to entice readers to buy your work, are essential.

This isn't to say that it's easy to write that sort of book description. It might even be the most difficult element to create for us authors.

Writing a novel is, by comparison, an artistic talent, after all. I get it. I've been there. However, we cannot ignore the business aspect of being an author. We have to sell books and in the online environment of today the book description is the gap between having your book drown in the sea of choices and having a sellable book that people want to read.

An effective blurb is not a book summary either. It's a catchy teaser, much like a movie trailer that gets us to go to the theater and buy a ticket to watch the whole film. The underlying philosophy of this entire book is to have a book description that is so effective that it convinces a person to exchange his or her hard-earned money, and time, to buy your book. It's really as simple as that.

To be honest, I should have learned how to get this right much sooner. There are so many examples of how new blurbs have led to a positive change in sales. When done right, the purchase of a book is almost automatic. Get it wrong, and almost nothing can save you. I will come back to this shortly in the chapter entitled, "How Important Are Book Descriptions Really?", with some hard-hitting data to defend my point of view.

I'm looking so much forward to teaching you all I have learned, so let's get to it. Just two short points to make first:

To avoid any confusion, I should mention that I'm using the words "book description" and "blurb" to mean the same thing. Traditionally, it wasn't so.

Back in the day, traditional publishing houses would call the line of praise, printed across the front cover of a book, the blurb. As publishing evolved over the years, authors have begun to use the term 'blurb' for a book description. Just know that, for simplicity reasons, I use the two interchangeably.

The other thing is: There is a difference between writing fiction and non-fiction blurbs. While the purpose is the same (to attract buyers) the methods are not.

In order not to leave you empty-handed, in case you are also writing non-fiction, I have included a bonus chapter towards the end of the book on how to write highly converting book descriptions for non-fiction books.

Alright. **It's time**… It's time to change your view of book descriptions. It's time to craft awesome blurbs. It's time to sell more books.

DISCLAIMER

everal factors play into selling novels. The content, the cover and the price point are all aspects that affect a reader's decision to buy a book.

A great cover won't make the sale on its own. Neither will an amazing book if it has a poor blurb and is expensive at the same time. It all needs to work together in harmony. Keep in mind, updating your blurb alone might not translate into increased sales. Perhaps you need to run paid advertising to get more eyeballs on your book? Do you need to update the cover? How about the content of the book itself: Is it up to scratch?

Keep in mind that in order to reap the benefits from this book, you *do* need to apply what you learn. When reading a non-fiction book, it's quite common to put it aside and make a mental note of how helpful it was. The reason we do this is most likely because it can feel overwhelming to figure everything out all at once.

To battle this, I have laid out the road to an awesome book description one brick at a time. You just need to follow along and do the work as you go. It won't get any easier than this.

And to make it even simpler: I have included a task list at the end of each chapter which summarizes what actions you need to take. This provides a simple and easy overview in the form of a check-list that you can clear before moving on to the next chapter.

HOW IMPORTANT ARE BOOK DESCRIPTIONS REALLY?

O ver the last few pages I have made claims on how important book descriptions are and how they can, and will, have a positive effect on revenue. I also promised to come back with some "hard-hitting data to defend my point of view".

In a world where thousands of new books are added to online book retailer sites every day, the number of choices made available to readers also keeps growing. Your book(s) is drowning in the pool and it matters little how well it's written. If nobody ever finds your book, they won't buy it either.

Nowadays, I can even loop books that are made available for free into this harsh reality. It's a crowded marketplace out there and without effective "sales techniques" (your book description is one of them), it's more than difficult to build an audience.

So why is it that I keep putting so much emphasis on the book description?

I don't like to make unsupported claims, so I looked to Mark Dawson – a bestselling indie author and marketing genius who I follow quite closely. He actually spent some time investigating this very topic and, because of all his success, he also has a very large reader base. He surveyed more than 10,000 people and asked what triggered each person to read his book: his cover, reviews, book title, etc.?

What he learned was that almost five times as many readers picked up his book because of the book description, as opposed to getting enticed by the cover. Giving the hype around book covers, I think this is very important and interesting information.

Imagine this scene: A fantasy fan is searching for the next book to read, either standing in the bookstore or scrolling through a screen full of offerings at online bookstores like Amazon. What catches his or her eye?

The book cover, of course. That's what piques the person's interest enough to pull it off the shelf, or click on it, to take a closer look.

As an author, you have spent money on that cover and it has now paid dividends. Well done.

Next up is the book description. It's these words that will decide whether or not you acquire a new reader.

One should think that lots of hard labor has gone into crafting that blurb, right?

Well, most book descriptions are just as horribly written as my own first blurb. (I will share it with you in a few chapters' time.) That's just a fact.

The good news is that writing strong blurbs that convert browsers into customers isn't some kind of secret formula that only the initiated are privileged to know. There is a structure to it, and by following the rules of my system, you will get better results, and steer clear of the common mistakes.

Do you recognize any of these? I know I have certainly been guilty of more than a few:

Mistake #1: Wordy descriptions

If readers are subjected to a wall of text that rambles on about this or that, they will assume the rest of the book to be more of the same.

A long blurb runs the risk of turning away a potential buyer.

Mistake #2: Telling too much

A blurb that reads more like a synopsis, revealing every major plot twist in the story, is a mistake.

You want the reader to read the story to learn all its secrets, not serving it to them upfront.

The book description is nothing but an open invitation to learn more.

Mistake #3: Fantasy words

We have some cool and unique names for our characters and places in a fantasy novel.

Dumping a whole load of them in the book description, thinking that it will help the reader understand who's who, is a big mistake.

As fantasy authors, we are often proud of our worldbuilding and want to show it off. This isn't the time for it.

The reader only needs to know a little.

Mistake #4: Using more than one narrative voice

In my research, I came across several instances where the book descriptions suddenly shifted from first person to third.

This is one <u>giant</u> no-no.

Mistake #5: Confusing teasers

You certainly do want to leave the reader wanting more after reading the blurb, but if you are too creative about it, all you'll do is confuse the reader. That's not going to translate into a sale.

There are times when it's worthwhile to be a bit cryptic. However, when it comes to blurbs, the presentation needs to be crisp and clear.

I hope you now have a better understanding of how undervalued book descriptions truly are. With that said, let's have a quick look at the mindset that you need to adopt.

You want to get straight into writing that awesome blurb, I understand, but stay with me for just a little while longer. There are a few important things to explain around mindset before we get too far ahead.

descriptions, it doesn't matter all that much anyway. We will just spend five minutes, whipping the blurb together, upload it, and leave it at that.

I want you to realize that we all have the power to become great copywriters.

What is holding the elephant back is also preventing us authors from writing better blurbs and selling more books. It's a prison of the mind.

You can break free by understanding the constraints we put upon ourselves. At the end of the day, copywriting is nothing but the mental process of getting your thoughts organized and then transferred onto paper or the screen. As in most cases, the best way to start, is to start.

The goal of the first draft it to put something – anything – on paper. Later you might add words, delete entire sentences or paragraphs, but that's all part of the copywriting process. It's what you do with the copy, after your first draft, that really makes the difference.

You will learn the techniques, step-by-step, which allow you to communicate why people should exchange their money for the pleasure of reading your book.

As earlier mentioned, the book description *isn't* the first step in the decision-making process to purchase a book, but it's the *most* important one.

You can do this!

THE READER IS KING

W e already discussed how readers browse websites, or bookstores, and how it's the cover and the title that draw them in first. With their interest piqued, they will read the blurb and go on to make their decisions from there. However, the thing I left out earlier is how buying a book is an emotional decision, rather than a logical one.

When searching for the next book to read, we look for what makes us feel excited, curious, enthusiastic, or moved. Rational thoughts, such as price, are a factor for obvious reasons, but the emotional play is pivotal. You want the reader to desire even more of your book.

If that's the name of the game, how do we achieve that?

In fantasy, like any other genre, readers will identify with the tropes of the genre. I mentioned how the human mind likes familiarity – well, it comes into play once again here. The key is to deliver an emotional stimulus that instantly connects with a fantasy fan. To this end, the character is the most important conduit. A character whom the reader can relate to or identify with, or who in some way seems similar to a character they liked from another book, or who just appeals to their sense of wanting to be the hero, is the best starting point.

You will learn how my formula always begins with the character and the aim to build that emotional connection with the reader. An analysis of all the reviews for the top 50 fantasy books on Amazon also revealed that the #1 reason readers liked a book was because of the characters. It was mentioned 7% more often than the plot being interesting or captivating.

Providing the reader with a character they can relate to just makes them feel comfortable. It confirms that this book is similar to what they have enjoyed before and it's therefore a safer bet.

We are creatures of habit and if you try to break the mold, if you attempt to stand out by having your blurb explain how different your book is, it's most likely that it will hurt your sales.

While multi-bestselling authors can do what they want and still sell a bazillion books, the same can't be said when you are starting out.

Focus your book description on what people want and it will serve you well.

That said, I also need to add a word of caution: Don't confuse the reader.

How many times have you picked up a book where the blurb gave you certain expectations, only to discover that the book wasn't delivering upon those promises. That's not the scenario I'm describing when I say, "focus your book description on what people want".

On the contrary. Your blurb is not supposed to appeal to every-one. In fact, it's better if it turns off those who are not fans of fantasy. Using words and tones that prevent, say, a sci-fi reader from picking up the book is important. Otherwise, you are more than likely to receive a one-star review in return.

Hence, it's in your own best interest to attract those who will like your book, rather than appealing to everyone out there – even if that means focusing only on a portion of the market. It might seem counter-intuitive, but having the reader being instantly able to tell what type of story they are getting is solid advice. In this context, the book description serves as a sort of gatekeeper.

This chapter is entitled "The Reader Is King", because that is what it's all about – fulfilling customer expectations. It can be hard for us authors to put ourselves in readers' shoes when we get caught up in delivering an enthralling story. We can forget that our customers are looking for entertainment and escapism.

"Turning the envelope over, his hand trembling, Harry saw a purple wax seal bearing a coat of arms; a lion, an eagle, a badger and a snake surrounding a larger letter 'H'."

"Harry Potter and the Philosopher's Stone" by J.K. Rowling
– Amazon Best Sellers Rank: #13 Paid in Kindle Store

That is a captivating book description! Given how we live in a *scanning culture* where 80% of us only stop to read the first line of the blurb, we have to deliver full impact instantly. Take no hostages.

I will circle back to all of this, and not only share insights into stylistic similarities we can draw upon from the bestselling fantasy books, but also give you a list of what I call '*Sovereign words*', which you can use to great effect when telegraphing to the reader that this is the book they are looking for.

We recognize these from when movies are advertised. You might recall, "In space, no one can hear your scream," from *Aliens*. Or perhaps closer to our fantasy hearts: "One ring to rule them all" – *The Lord of the Rings*.

The purpose of these tag lines is, in just a few words, to give the audience a sense of what they are in for.

Let's look at two examples from among bestselling fantasy books:

"The gods walk again."

"War God's Mantle" by James Hunter
– Amazon Best Sellers Rank: #1,138 Paid in Kindle Store

Or:

"There is no cure for being who you really are..."

"The Mermaid's Sister" by Carrie Anne Noble
– Amazon Best Sellers Rank: #203 Paid in Kindle Store

In creating the tag line, it will sometimes hit you like a bolt of lightning and in other cases, you will have to work harder at it.

In both cases, learn to love tag lines. Pay attention to them. Develop your skills and craft some truly attention-grabbing ones.

Step 2. Character introduction

Earlier on, I mentioned how you should always begin the blurb with the character and build the emotional connection with the reader. Then I proceeded to spring the tag line on you...

My apologies, but step 2 is in fact where the *real* book description begins – with the character (one character, not several). The reader needs to know who they are going to meet and why that particular character deserves attention.

Although the tag line *is* an incredibly important attention-grabber, the first sentence you use to introduce your main character is too. Its primary job is to be read and to keep the audience engaged. Fail at this and you lose the sale.

So, if this first sentence is vital, what can you do to make it compelling enough to pique the reader's interest?

The answer: Make it short.

It needs to be so concise and easy to read that your reader is sucked into it. Think of a freight ship. It works really hard as it fires up its propulsion system. The amount of energy and engagement required to get the boat moving is enormous. But once it is pushing its way across the water, it becomes easier and easier. The same can be said for step 2.

Your first sentence should be compelling by the merit of its short length and ease of reading. Therefore, be mindful that you don't include any of our wonderful, yet strange fantasy words right off the bat.

"My name is Kvothe. I have stolen princesses back from sleeping barrow kings."

"The Name of the Wind" by Patrick Rothfuss
– Amazon Best Sellers Rank: #36,583 Paid in Kindle Store

Or:

"Fourteen-year-old Augum grew up with bullies instead of friends."

"The only way to find the traitor, keep her secrets, and save those she loves is to raise her blade against the Holy warriors of God, shattering the Vatican itself."

"Whispers" by Shayne Silvers
– Amazon Best Sellers Rank: #1,022 Paid in Kindle Store

Step 5. Dire Straits and Call to Action

Step 5 is the hook at the end. By raising the danger of the main character not achieving his or her goal, you are creating a cliffhanger that engages the reader emotionally.

"Frodo must leave his home and make a perilous journey across Middle-earth to the Cracks of Doom, there to destroy the Ring and foil the Dark Lord in his evil purpose."

"The Fellowship of the Ring" by J.R.R. Tolkien
– Amazon Best Sellers Rank: #124,521 Paid in Kindle Store

Or:

"Unless all the nations of Roshar can put Dalinar's blood-soaked past aside and stand together – and unless Dalinar himself can confront the past – even the restoration of the Knights Radiant will not avert the end of civilization."

"Oathbringer" by Brandon Sanderson
– Amazon Best Sellers Rank: #15,511 Paid in Kindle Store

You are attempting to lure the reader into wanting more. End with something meaningful and strong.

When you have the reader's attention, right here, where their eyes are resting on an impactful final word, that's when you transition into the *call to action*.

A *call to action* is marketing language for a command that explains to the reader what they should do next. It's the selling paragraph that concludes the transaction and ensures that the reader does what you want them to do. I prefer to be subtle about it by saying something like, "Click Download Free Sample". More on that later, as we get into the detailed description of step 5.

Calls to action are effective. For this reason, you need to add one to the end of your book description.

I highlighted how this formula will make your life easier when it comes to writing blurbs. I should also point out that following the formula to the letter isn't necessarily always the answer. When the need calls for it, feel free to adapt the steps and make them your own.

WHAT NOT TO DO

I n relaying "what not to do", it's often a good idea to begin with an example. Analyzing it and highlighting what went wrong is an approach I find solidifies the "what to do" much stronger.

At this point, I have talked you through the elements that make up a well-crafted book description. While I have shared some snippet examples in pages past, I haven't really ventured into much detail. In other words, you are missing the *how to* parts. Given that this is why you purchased this book in the first place, we better get moving…

I'm going to share one of my earlier blurbs of *Desolation* (book 1 in my epic fantasy trilogy). While it might not be the worst blurb you have ever read, I do believe that it won't make you think, "Oh my God. I just have to get this book."

So, here it is in its entirety:

Just as Aea had finally found happiness in her troubled life, everything starts to fall apart. When she discovers that her sister is still alive Aea ventures to save her, well aware that every Duian who leaves the forest realm of Thaduin will inevitably catch a deadly disease, the Field Blight. Aea finds herself in a race against time.

Meanwhile, Ayida, another Duian, resides in the Bronze Tower, far north of Thaduin, where she has grown to become a powerful spellcaster. However, it requires all of her skills to heal herself of the Field Blight daily. This place is the heart of the Magio Order, a powerful organization of female magic wielders, where Ayida has tried for decades to ascend from Apprentice to the rank of Sienna... and failed every time.

Will the world of Erisdün survive as myth and reality become one?

"Desolation" is the first book in the fantasy trilogy, "The Keystone Bone". It's not for the faint-hearted, but if you like fast-paced fantasy, with dragons, demons, and magic, then you will love "Desolation".

Download today and experience a struggle like no other.

If this blurb didn't move you, I don't blame you.

At the time I thought it was pretty good. I don't anymore – it doesn't stir the reader's emotions in any way and thus falls short of its purpose. However, it is on a par with many other book descriptions out there, which means that there is fertile ground to make your blurb stand apart.

Since we have just gone through the *5 Steps to Great Blurbs*, what better way than to use that as our lens in taking a closer look at this book description. Where does it fail? Along the way, I will add some commentary on what not to do.

Step 1. Tag line

My blurb didn't even have a tag line. No attention grabber what so ever. I'm not sure what else to say…

Step 2. Character introduction

On a good note: That first line is relatively short, so that's not too bad. It also introduces a sense of wonder in the reader, making the person curious as to why everything is falling apart. The problem lies after that first line.

Before going there, notice how I managed to limit myself to addressing Aea by her first name only. It's not uncommon, especially in fantasy, to see full names and titles being put on display. This bogs down the flow of the blurb, so avoid it.

Alright, so the second paragraph proceeds to mention another character, Ayida. This might not be a mistake in itself, as she is an integral part of the story, but if you find yourself in a situation where you want to mention more than two characters in the blurb, you might be heading for troubled waters. Turn back and rethink how you are building the book description.

What happened in this case was that I jumped straight into talking about Ayida and the plot that revolves around her. I completely neglected to share either of the characters' goals and motivations. On a good day, I might be able to argue that I skimmed the surface on that one, but the blurb never gets to the heart of the matter.

Step 3. Inciting Incident

The inciting incident… if you reread the blurb, can you tell where it is?

It's in fact this sentence: *"When she discovers that her sister is still alive Aea ventures to save her."*

I'm not particular happy with the delivery here. The inciting incident has no punch to it and is almost mentioned in passing. That is no way to treat such an important element.

In the previous chapter, I mentioned how this section of the blurb is where you need to be careful not to go bonkers with the backstory. I didn't exactly avoid that death trap myself, so it's important to reiterate that there is no need for a full primer to new readers. To this end, both worldbuilding and character history can be a problem.

As a rule of thumb: You need far less than you think.

Half a sentence to offer context, can work greater wonders than two full sentences with details on setting. In fact, in many cases you can get by without even mentioning where the book is taking place.

Step 4. Escalate tension

Instead of escalating the tension, I derailed into worldbuilding. I mention the Duians, Thaduin, the Field Blight, the Bronze Tower, the Magio Order, Apprentices and Siennas. Tired yet? Confused?

While some of these names and terminologies might be important to the plot, and thus deserve a place in the blurb, I certainly didn't need to include all of them.

As fantasy authors, this is our vice. Please… please… please… fight your instinct and focus on escalating the tension, rather than explaining your fantastical world.

In general, try and keep the details of your world a bit vague. Otherwise, you will end up wasting precious words explaining concepts that will only hamper what could have been an interesting book description.

Your book sales will thank you for it.

Step 5. Dire Straits and Call to Action

My blurb does at least attempt to create a cliffhanger, *"Will the world of Erisdün survive as myth and reality become one?"*

clicks away and becomes a reader of another author instead. Spend every word by focusing on the protagonist's journey.

Warnings

From time to time, authors want to warn readers at the end of the blurb. It could be a warning about content that may trigger a negative response in some readers or that the book might make the reader feel uncomfortable.

In most cases such warnings are unnecessary, but if your book does require one, consider using the phrase, "Author's Note" or "Alert". The word "Warning" is a heavy hitter and best avoided.

Did you notice how I have skillfully avoided the most frequently asked question? The one asking: "How long should a book description be?"

Don't worry about that for now. Once we get into the editing phase, I will tell you.

Without further ado, let's get into the weeds and write some book descriptions.

As we go, I'm going to write a completely new blurb for *Desolation*. Allow me to make it clear: My aim isn't to use the creation of this new blurb to make you interested in buying *Desolation*. It's only a way of allowing you to look over my shoulder as I apply the techniques of this book step by step.

WRITING THE BOOK DESCRIPTION

STEP 1: TAG LINE

The term 'tag line' varies depending on the country. I'm using the U.S. terminology for this one-liner that sums up a key aspect or theme of the book. In the U.K. these are referred to as 'end lines' or 'straplines'.

Since many browse the Internet on tablets and phones these days, there is no way of knowing how much of your full book description shows up on each type of device. Having a strong tag line is what ensures the appetizer.

As covered, we thus need to ensure that the tag line grabs the reader's attention. In order to do this, it needs to be short, catchy and memorable. It's like the slogan you would see on a movie poster – done wrong, you immediately lose the sale, rendering the rest of the blurb obsolete.

It might seem daunting to write a single line with the aim of making such a powerful first impression that it draws people in. How do we even determine what the book is truly about? How do we know what the theme is?

While tag lines *are* tough to generate, just thinking of one is a great starting point. So, to prime your mind on writing the rest of the blurb, imagine that your book is being turned into a movie... See... that already made you feel better. I'm joking, but play along here.

You are now the person in charge of writing the line that the bass-heavy, male voice-over actor at the end of the trailer is supposed to read out loud. It's those "In a world..." sentences that boom out through the loudspeakers in the theater.

To do this well, you aren't looking to explain the plot of the movie. Your only job is to hook people so they will go and purchase a ticket to see this blockbuster. Working on something this important can even make the best of us shiver with nervousness. Tell yourself that you can do this. Take a deep breath if it helps to get into the right frame of mind, then focus on your book...

Think of the three most compelling aspects of the book. They are most likely hidden among these: plot, setting, characters, and/or conflict.

Write them down.

Example, Desolation

> 1. Demons threatening the world
> 2. Aea risking the life of her unborn child
> 3. Friendship and doing what is right

These aren't tag line ideas. They are merely a way of focusing on writing one. Before we get that far, though, it's well worth evaluating what was just created.

Take a look at your three aspects and consider if the essence of your book has been captured. Look beyond the words, scrutinize whether or not you think that the aspect you have settled on is robust enough to attract the attention of a busy reader.

In my own assessment, I don't think that #3, "Friendship and doing what is right", has enough tenacity to it. Alright, it has to go. I will have to come up with something that can beat it. Let's see:

3. The servants of an ancient dragon invading the world

That's much better.

With the three aspects locked in, it's time to develop the actual tag line.

Now, based on each of the three aspects, write five different sentences. Or in other words, write five sentences per aspect. It will give you a total of fifteen different tag lines. Remember, these tag lines need to resonate with fantasy readers and at the same time match the tone of your book. If your book is humorous, then try to catch some of that essence in the tag line. If your book is dark, then use the tag line to demonstrate it.

Don't worry too much about making the sentences sound perfect at this stage. We will get to that in a minute.

Aspect #1, Demons threatening the world

1. When the world thought itself safe, the demons returned
2. An ancient evil awakens
3. After eons of imprisonment, the Arch Demon is about to break free
4. An all-powerful demon is about to unleash hell
5. A magical barrier is all that stands between the ancient demon and the fate of the world

Aspect #2, Aea risking the life of her unborn child

1. Which is worth more: the life of your unborn child or that of your sister?
2. Would you risk the life of your unborn child to save your sister?
3. In a race against time, the life of Aea's unborn child hangs in the balance
4. In a daring attempt to save her sister, Aea puts the life of her unborn at risk
5. The clock is ticking. If Aea doesn't save her sister soon, she will lose not only her unborn child, but also her own life

Aspect #3, The servants of an ancient dragon invading the world

1. The ancient dragon was believed to be nothing but a legend
2. Eons ago, the dragon and its army were defeated. That is all about to change
3. In search of the legendary Keystone Bone, an ancient dragon dispatches its army
4. The legendary dragon is forced into a wild chase for the Keystone Bone
5. As the ancient dragon begins its search for the Keystone Bone the fate of the world hangs in the balance

Wow. There is a lot of potential in here; however, it needs polishing. Rarely will you come up with a tag line that grabs the reader, and holds them tight, straight away.

Next, merge each of the five different versions into one. You are looking to condense the list of possible tag lines to only three, one per aspect.

In writing these, use short words. See if you can create contrast or twist the meaning of words. Don't use character names. Surprise the reader and enthrall them by strategic placement of Sovereign words (flip to Appendix B) for maximum impact. Don't become convoluted in a mad attempt to make it sound unique, though. It needs to flow and be as easy to read as possible.

Use no more than 15 words per tag line, craft one compelling tag line per aspect.

Aspect #1, Demons threatening the world

The ancient demon plots revenge: Armageddon awaits.

Aspect #2, Aea risking the life of her unborn child

Would you rescue your sister if it placed your unborn child in the balance?

Aspect #3, The servants of an ancient dragon invading the world

Eons have turned the great dragon into legend. Tales soon become disastrously real...

These are now your prime candidates for the final tag line. As a sanity check, look each one over and make sure that none of them are misleading. Verify that they reflect the content of your book.

Are you happy with what you came up with? If not, keep tweaking until you are completely satisfied, because next it's time to ask your fans to choose their favorite.

In order to ease the burden of collecting responses, I create a Google Form in which people can vote for their favorite tag line. Google Forms are completely free to use, but you can obviously also create a poll on Facebook, or even do it manually by asking people to respond to you directly.

So, send out an email to your list, post it to a Facebook group, on social media, or however you are reaching your fans – as long as you make sure that you are funneling readers of fantasy to the survey. If not, the data will get skewed. A romance reader will get excited by a different type of tag line than what strikes a chord with your intended audience.

Speaking of statistical research, the more responses you can garner, the merrier. Getting ten people to share their opinion is, without a doubt, better than basing the decision on your own preferences. However, in comparison, hundreds of votes ensure that you haven't accidentally asked a subset of the market and end up concluding a winning tag line that doesn't truly appeal to most.

Five days after posting the link to my Google Form, I reviewed the 113 responses. This is what I learned:

- 30,1% preferred: "The ancient demon plots revenge: Armageddon awaits"
- 30,1% preferred: "Would you rescue your sister if it placed your unborn child in the balance?"
- 39,8% preferred: "Eons have turned the great dragon into legend. Tales soon become disastrously real..."

With 39,8% of the votes, I have found my tag line.

Task List

- Take note of the three most compelling aspects of your book
- Expand upon these aspects by writing five different sentences as potential tag lines
- Boil down the five tag lines into one for each aspect
- Survey your audience and ask them to vote for their favorite among the three final tag lines

- Review results and conclude on the tag line for your book

STEP 2: CHARACTER INTRODUCTION

Introducing the character is where the book description really begins. While the tag line was strong enough to capture attention, this is where you want to build a connection with the reader. When we read a blurb, we *want* to find something that interests us. We *want* to get to know a character we can relate to.

Here in Step 2, we are going to write a short paragraph, no more than three sentences long, allowing the main character to step onto the stage.

In fantasy, though, we often have lots of characters and multiple points of view. This is an innate problem that could end up overwhelming the reader. A long list of characters won't build the character intimacy we are looking for. Instead, you need to clue the customer in on the main protagonist. How do we decide who the main protagonist is, then?

Often one or two characters will dominate the story. They will have more chapters devoted to their point of view than the rest of the cast. This is a clear telltale sign that you are dealing with a main character. If that is not the case, consider who we meet in the first chapter. This will more often than not be one of the most important characters.

Decide who the main hero is in your story because all good adventures are about a character. In that sense, it matters little if we are dealing with a human, a vampire, or something else. Any of those could be the person you want to shine the light on.

"On the evening of Sofia Claremont's seventeenth birthday, she is sucked into a nightmare from which she cannot wake."

"A Shade of Vampire" by Bella Forest
— Amazon Best Sellers Rank: #404 Paid in Kindle Store

The above example is the strongest character introduction I could find among the bestselling fantasy books on Amazon. It does several things really, really well. Notice how it focuses on conflict, without subjecting us to detailed exposition. It zooms in on the beginning scenario which the main character finds herself in. It introduces Sofia by name and we learn one relevant detail about the character, and that is that she has just turned seventeen.

Here is a short checklist of what the Character Introduction paragraph needs to include:

- Focus on conflict
- Name the character
- Share one relevant detail about the character
- The first sentence should be short and easy to read
- No more than three sentences long

45

Focusing on conflict

Conflict begins with the character's primal need and the goal that drives this person forward. It will be something so important that the character will risk everything to achieve his or her goal.

At its core, it's topics such as: Love, Understanding, Subsistence, Protection, Participation, Identity, Freedom.

What you need to uncover is which "fundamental want" (it doesn't have to be one of those mentioned above) is relevant for your particular novel and how it plays out in the beginning chapters. The conflict can be both internal and external, but the external is more often notable when it comes to book descriptions. It's all the things that can get in your character's way as they attempt to achieve their goal. It's obstacles. The risks that need to be taken. Or the consequences of failure.

Here is a method that will help you distill what type of conflict to focus on, but please, don't follow it slavishly. Use it as a tool and adapt as necessary.

Fill in the following sentence: Character wants [goal] because [motivation] but [conflict] prevents it.

Example, *Desolation*

Aea wants [to save her sister] because [she misses her family] but [leaving the forest subjects her to the deadly disease, the Field Blight].

Name the character

The key is to bond the reader to your character, and knowing someone by name is the first step in that process. While the Amazon bestseller I just shared named Sofia by her last name, my general advice is to only use the person's first name. There is no need to add last names unless you have a compelling reason to do so.

Sharing one relevant detail

In deciding what detail to share, find one that is integral to the character's story. In a blurb no one cares if the hero is blue-eyed or has blond hair, or how old he or she is. I know the bestseller example spoke of the character's age, too. That is a trope of the Young Adult (YA) genre, so the author did the right thing there.

What matters is the character's role in the story. In fantasy, this can often mean focusing on the person's race or species, what tribe the protagonist belongs to, perhaps something that portrays rank, relationship or a notable characteristic, such as war veteran.

Sticking with the basics is often the best approach. In doing so, you should also notice how the headline of this section contains the word *relevant*. So, don't overwhelm the reader. You are looking to paint a very brief picture of the character, nothing more.

Example, *Desolation*

Pregnant, outsider or misfit

Author's note: Aea is of a race called Duian. I chose not to add that detail to the list of relevant details. If I had, I would be breaking my own commandment that there should be no strange words in the character introduction. If your novel portrays elves or vampires, just to name two examples, they are considered tropes and readers will instantly understand what it is. In such cases there is nothing wrong with using this as your relevant detail.

Writing the Character Introduction – Example, Desolation

To summarize, these are my building blocks:

- Conflict – Aea wants [to save her sister] because [she misses her family] but [leaving the forest subjects her to the deadly disease, the Field Blight].
- Name of the character: Aea
- One relevant detail: pregnant, outsider or misfit.

I can now write the first part of my blurb, the character introduction. As mentioned, I need to make the first sentence short and easy to read and this whole paragraph is to be no longer than three sentences.

Example, *Desolation*

Aea is an outsider. The clan executed her father when she was only six years old. Her mother and older sister left for unknown reasons, never to return.

By making the character introduction appeal to general human emotions and desires, you will start off your blurb in the best of ways.

Task List

- Fill in the sentence mentioned under *Focusing on conflict* to make the conflict stand clear in your mind

- Decide on only using the first name for the character, or also including the last name
- Make a note of one relevant detail to share about the character, but avoid any "fantasy-heavy" words
- Pull these different inputs together. Write no more than three lines to introduce the character. Remember to keep the first line short and easy to read

STEP 3: INCITING INCIDENT

W hen Gandalf comes rolling into the Shire on his cart, the story begins. In The Lord of the Rings, we were first introduced to the Hobbits and then the arrival of the wizard, marking the inciting incident.

This Step 3 works in much the same way. While in Step 2, we had the character introduction (we got to know the Hobbits), now it's time to add the single plot point that propels your story into motion.

> **"In a sleepy village in the Shire, young Frodo Baggins finds himself faced with an immense task, as his elderly cousin Bilbo entrusts the Ring to his care."**
>
> *"The Fellowship of the Ring" by J.R.R. Tolkien*
> *– Amazon Best Sellers Rank: #75,640 Paid in Kindle Store*

As this example shows, we are not being told the multitude of plot points that make up *The Lord of the Rings*. Instead, the inciting incident is brought to the forefront and forms the most essential part of the blurb.

You might be thinking, "But how does this map to the character introduction, I just wrote in Step 2?"

We will merge all the pieces together in the end. For now, just perceive each of these steps as isolated building blocks and instead decide what the hook is in your novel. What is the inciting incident that should be included in the book description? It could be a big revelation, like Frodo receiving the Ring. It could be that someone is on the run. Perhaps a surprising turn of events is uncovered?

In a few moments, we are going to write a maximum of three sentences about the inciting incident, but allow me to offer some guidance first.

Up until this point, I have told you to hold back on the fantasy elements. I have advised how ease of reading trumps everything else. Well, you can now loosen the reins a bit.

The uniqueness of a fantasy world can be an appealing point to readers of fantasy. As you have likely already guessed, the introduction of places, people or species needs to be tied to the inciting incident. Derailing your book description by naming a bunch of different places or additional characters will do you no good. As always, the magic formula is to keep it relevant. That said, stating something about the setting can sometimes work wonders and add a whole new layer to the blurb. Consider for a moment: Do you have a hidden gem in your worldbuilding that could serve well as a little spice on top? Nothing more than that: we don't want to drown the reader in descriptors.

Alright, I need to come back to something I said earlier, in order to set up this next piece of advice correctly. Back in the chapter, *5 Steps to Great Blurbs*, I wrote: "It will strengthen the book description significantly if you can include a twist or a circumstance, that forces a transformation on the character while conveying the heart of the story."

When it comes to the inciting incident the trick becomes to ensure that it relates to the character. Don't choose an inciting incident that in no way affects our hero. Here are a few ways in which you can effectively tie the two together:

1. The word "When" is often a go-to solution. For example, "When the dragon awakes from its slumber…", "When a mysterious parchment reveals an ancient secret…" or "When the old wizard arrives…"
2. The word "In" is another option. For example, "In a sleepy village…", "In a long forgotten realm…", "In the far corners of the world…"
3. The word "To" is yet another choice at your disposal. For example, "To win back her lost love…", "To save her sister…", "To discover the secret of…."

Your guiding star is to always leave the reader begging to learn what happens next. The inciting incident informs of how the story begins and at the same time invites the potential buyer to join the journey.

It's time to apply what we have just covered, so go ahead and write your inciting incident.

Example, *Desolation*

When her mother suddenly turns up, broken by the deadly disease the Field Blight, Aea faces a desperate choice.

Leaving the protective forest realm to save her lost sister involves subjecting herself, and her unborn child, to the Field Blight.

Aware of her sister being in mortal danger, Aea gambles
everything in a race against time.

These sentences still need a bit of work, but don't worry about
that. At the moment, as I said, these are merely building blocks.
We are going to polish it into a diamond later on.

Task List

- Decide upon the inciting incident to include in the blurb
- Consider if you have a unique setting descriptor that will
  enhance the blurb
- Tie the inciting incident to the character
- Write the inciting incident in three sentences or less

STEP 4: ESCALATE TENSION

I have mentioned it a few times already, but that is because it's so important. This Step 4 is offering yet another temptation to begin adding subplots to the book description.

Doing so won't deepen your blurb. A new place name, or unrelated character, won't make it more interesting. Instead, *Escalating Tension* only refers to the protagonist's journey. Stick with the character you have worked so hard to introduce and show just how bad things are truly going to get.

Allow me to explain by example. Here is the next part of the blurb that I shared in Step 3, from The Lord of the Rings:

"Frodo must leave his home and make a perilous journey across Middle-earth to the Cracks of Doom, there to destroy the Ring and foil the Dark Lord in his evil purpose."

"The Fellowship of the Ring" by J.R.R. Tolkien
– Amazon Best Sellers Rank: #75,640 Paid in Kindle Store

You see what I mean? The anchor is Frodo. We are indeed told of Middle-earth, the Cracks of Doom and a Dark Lord. However, it's done by talking about Frodo. None of the other Hobbits are even mentioned.

One more thing and then it's time for you to complete Step 4 of your book description. Notice how this example raises a question:

"Can the choices she makes in the present override supernatural ties and legends of old? Or is her future already written in stone?"

"Dark Side of the Moon" by Rachel Jonas
– Amazon Best Sellers Rank: #1,470 Paid in Kindle Store

Wouldn't it sound better if the above example had read, "How can the choices she makes in the present override supernatural ties and legends of old?"? Of all the emotions a blurb can arouse in the reader, curiosity is the most powerful one. In escalating the tension, try to include a question by using a "how" question. This ensures that it can't be answered by a simple yes or no.

It's now time to add the next building block to your blurb. In your book, what happens after the inciting incident? Does it tie in with the main character? If not, explore further. Find the next beat that directly affects the protagonist.

Once you've got it, write no more than three lines, in which you escalate the tension and, if you can, end it with a "how" question.

Example, *Desolation*

Outside the forest, the world of Erisdün is nothing like Aea had ever imagined.

How will she survive when she realizes that the Field Blight might be the least of her concerns?

Task List

- Decide what plot element makes things worse for the main character
- Escalate the tension by writing no more than three sentences
- If you can, end with a "how" question

STEP 5: DIRE STRAITS AND CALL TO ACTION

W ell done. You have now reached the final part of the book description and I hope you already recognize how your blurb is much stronger than it used to be.

Step 5 is what I call Dire Straits.

This is the low point. The part where things get so bad that the character cannot possibly survive or get out of the whole ordeal. You are obviously not going to reveal the ending of your novel, or give away any twists or surprises. The Dire Straits center on the character and will in most cases have something to do with the main climax of your book. Try to identify the ultimate evil or the painstaking consequence of failure.

Once you have decided what it is, write the dire straits in three sentences or less.

As always, examples speak more than a thousand words:

"If he fails, the kingdom will be ripped apart, and Rezkin will have violated Rule 1 – to protect and honor his friends – leaving him without country, purpose, or honor."

"Legends of Ahn" by Kel Kade
– Amazon Best Sellers Rank: #2,747 Paid in Kindle Store

"Each step closer to the truth takes Ethan further from the world he thought he knew, from the man he thought he was, until he must face a horrifying fact – he may never get out of the Wayward Pines alive."

"Pines" by Blake Crouch
– Amazon Best Sellers Rank: #2,598 Paid in Kindle Store

"But as Trip will soon discover, what he thought he knew about himself is only a shadow of the truth. Reality is far more incredible than he ever imagined."

"Revelations" by Lindsay Buroker
– Amazon Best Sellers Rank: #911 Paid in Kindle Store

Example, *Desolation*

Ancient myths become reality as the great dragon dispatches his army to retrieve the Keystone Bone – the bone of a God, the only component to prevent the Arch Demon from breaking free.

Forces, as old as time itself, make Aea's journey more perilous than ever.

Perfect. The draft of your blurb is now done. You deserve a break and something to enjoy.

Writing a book description is far from easy and you will pleased to know that the hard part is now over. In coming chapters, you still need to edit it, but the entire structure is now in place, so it merely becomes a matter of polishing.

Before getting that far, though, you still need to augment the book description with a call to action.

If the blurb did its job, as it should, then the reader is now hovering his or her mouse over the buy button. The call to action is the selling paragraph that affirms to the reader what genre the book belongs to, which volume it might be in a series and why the reader will like it. It's simply what makes the reader click and purchase your book.

Compared to what you have gone through so far, the call to action is incredibly simple to create.

The formula for books in a series goes like this:

[Book title] is a [fantasy subgenre].

If you like [insert what best describes your book the most – it might be one of these or something different: Adventure? Deep characters? Fast-paced? Fantastic worlds?] then you will love [book title].

[A subtle call to action, like "Click 'Download Free Sample' and enjoy." Or, "Discover the exciting adventure today"]

This is the [book's placement in the series, i.e. first] installment in the [series name]. [Optional: if the books must be read in order, you might want to state: "(Must be read in order)"]

[Optional: If your book has lots of reviews, you might add a sentence saying, "Over X worldwide reviews." Or add excerpts if any renowned media or authors have reviewed your book.]

The formula for standalone books goes like this:

[book title] is a [fantasy subgenre].

If you like [insert what best describes your book the most – it might be one of these or something different: Adventure? Deep characters? Fast-paced? Fantastic worlds?] then you will love [book title].

[A subtle call to action, like, "Click 'Download Free Sample' and enjoy." Or, "Discover the exciting adventure today"]

[Optional: If your book has lots of reviews, you might add a sentence saying, "Over X worldwide reviews." Or add excerpts if any renowned media or authors have reviewed your book.]

Example, *Desolation*

Desolation is an epic fantasy.

If you like a fast-paced read with dragons and demons, then you will love *Desolation*.

Delve into the exciting adventure today.

This is the first book in the *Keystone Bone* trilogy.
(Must be read in order)

Task List

- Decide what constitutes dire straits for the main character
- In adding the description of dire straits to the blurb, use no more than three sentences
- Include a call to action at the end of your blurb

PUTTING THE BLURB TOGETHER

S ince we are going to edit the blurb next, we need all the building blocks combined into one.

Example, *Desolation*

Eons have turned the great dragon into legend. Tales soon become disastrously real…

Aea is an outsider. The clan executed her father when she was only six years old. Her mother and older sister left for unknown reasons, never to return.

When her mother suddenly turns up, broken by the deadly disease the Field Blight, Aea faces a desperate choice.

Leaving the protective forest realm to save her lost sister involves subjecting herself, and her unborn child, to the Field Blight.

Aware of her sister being in mortal danger, Aea gambles everything in a race against time.

Outside the forest, the world of Erisdün is nothing like Aea had ever imagined.

How will she survive when she realizes that the Field Blight might be the least of her concerns?

Ancient myths become reality as the great dragon dispatches his army to retrieve the Keystone Bone – the bone of a God, the only component to prevent the Arch Demon from breaking free.

Forces, as old as time itself, makes Aea's journey more perilous than ever.

Desolation is an epic fantasy.

If you like a fast-paced read with dragons and demons, then you will love *Desolation*.

Delve into the exciting adventure today.

This is the first book in the *Keystone Bone* trilogy.
(Must be read in order)

Start by splicing together the tag line, the character introduction, the inciting incident, the escalate tension section, the dire straits and the call to action. You might need to change a few words, but remember, all you are trying to accomplish is to create a cohesive whole. Don't obsess over making it sound perfect.

Example, *Desolation*

Eons have turned the great dragon into legend. Tales soon become disastrously real…

Aea is an outsider. The clan executed her father when she was only six years old. Her mother and older sister left for unknown reasons, never to return.

When her mother suddenly turns up, broken by the deadly disease the Field Blight, Aea faces a desperate decision. Leaving the protective forest realm to save her lost sister involves subjecting herself, and her unborn child, to the Field Blight.

Aware of her sister being in mortal danger, Aea gambles everything in a race against time. But, outside the forest, the world of Erisdün is nothing like Aea had ever imagined.

How will she survive when she realizes that the Field Blight might be the least of her concerns? When ancient myths become reality by the great dragon dispatching his army to retrieve the Keystone Bone – the bone of a God, the only component to prevent the Arch Demon from breaking free.

Forces, as old as time itself, make Aea's journey more perilous than ever.

Desolation is an epic fantasy.

If you like a fast-paced read with dragons and demons, then you will love *Desolation*.

Delve into the exciting adventure today.

This is the first book in the *Keystone Bone* trilogy. (Must be read in order)

Task List

- Tie the sentences together into a cohesive whole. Don't fuzz over it. Editing is up next

EDITING THE BOOK DESCRIPTION

WHERE TO BEGIN?

W ith the draft of the book description at hand – that unpolished diamond – these next chapters are what will make it shine.

Up until this point, your main concern has been to identify the building blocks that, when joined together, make up the blurb. It makes absolutely no difference if what you have at this stage sounds awful. The important thing is that you picked the content carefully and made it to invoke curiosity and other emotions in the reader. If so, you have mastered a very important technique.

The emotion comes from the words themselves, and sometimes changing a single word will increase the effectiveness of the book description. That's not to say that you have to understand the emotional impact of every word in order to write a great blurb. Rather, view it as general knowledge that you will acquire over time.

To assist you along the way are coming chapters on editing.

This process has been divided into three different phases. In each phase, you are going to go over the book description, making it better and stronger. I recommend that you complete these three phases in order as they have been designed to first correct the fundamentals before drilling down towards the minute details.

Once that is done, some information will follow about formatting, but you are already closer than ever to having a completely new book description for your book.

PHASE 1: TRIMMING

I n editing the book description, the very first thing I will ask of you is to see yourself as a publisher. At this stage, you are no longer the author, editing your own work. Instead, making an impact on the reader is your principal concern and the blurb is a piece of marketing material, nothing else.

Think of it this way: The three phases of editing aren't supposed to be approached with your heart, but with your head.

I called this first phase *trimming*.

Let me return to the frequently asked question that I've dodged so far. It was this one: "How long should a book description be?"

I will answer this question in a second and also give you the tools to complete the *trimming*. Along the way, I will edit my example blurb and explain why I'm making the choices that I do. My hope is that this will make the theory more applicable.

Alright, that question… without enough description, you won't be able to deliver the emotional impact you're striving for, but on the other hand, too much description will bore the reader to death.

That Amazon allows you to spend 2,000 words on your book description certainly doesn't mean that you should do so.

Besides, a shorter blurb is also a safeguard for the printed version of your book. If you use Amazon's CreateSpace™ – or similar print-on-demand services – to produce paperbacks, then you will want your text to fit well on the back cover.

While fantasy readers do expect slightly more description than, say, a thriller reader, it's always a wise choice not to assault the reader with a block of text. That said, the fact that your blurb is emotionally impacting will always be more important than how long the book description is.

I know that you are looking for a definite number, though. If I have to give you one, I will say: Keep your blurb under 300 words in total.

A quick check of my example description for *Desolation* tells me that it currently sits at 219 words. I'm pretty happy with that. Less is often more, so let's get into trimming.

1. Repetition

The easiest place to start is to look for areas where you might be repeating yourself.

As just mentioned, you are writing a piece of marketing material. It needs to read like professional ad copy, and stating the same plot point twice, even with different words, is something you can easily get rid of. In most cases, you can simply remove it without impacting the blurb as a whole. If deletion proves difficult, consider how you can rephrase the sentence in a way where it carries more emotion instead of plot description.

Check your draft.

Any repetition you can cut?

2. Simplify

Only the most essential details should form part of the final blurb. We fantasy authors are used to writing very long books, but that's a luxury you don't have when it comes to book descriptions. I suppose that's a fact that shouldn't come as a surprise at this point.

Perhaps you have a whole sentence that could be taken out without hurting the overall narrative? It could be that some phrases are too complicated and could be simplified not to slow the reader down. The more the reader is asked to work in order to understand your descriptions, the worse it is.

Rewriting characters or descriptions in a less flowery way can often drastically decrease your word count. Look for ways to remove unnecessary explanations and/or simplify what you have written. Can you explain the same thing in fewer words?

The shorter the blurb, the more impact it will have. This means that every word counts.

I have included the *Desolation* example, in its changed form, at the end of this chapter, but in summary here's what I changed:

- "The clan executed her father when she was only six years old." Changed to: "At age six, the clan executed her father."

This new sentence explains the exact same thing as the previous, but it only uses eight words instead of twelve.

- "When her mother suddenly turns up." Changed to: "When her mother suddenly appears."

Another word removed.

- "Leaving the protective forest realm to save her lost sister involves subjecting herself, and her unborn child, to the Field Blight. Aware of her sister being in mortal danger, Aea gambles everything in a race against time." Changed to: "Rescuing her sister from mortal danger involves leaving the protective forest realm and subjecting herself – and her unborn child – to the Field Blight. A race against time has begun."

This change, not only reduced from 36 to 29 words, but in the process also made the sentences a lot clearer.

- "Outside the forest, the world of Erisdün is nothing like Aea had ever imagined." Changed to: "The world of Erisdün is nothing like Aea had imagined."

Again, simplified and removed four more words.

- "How will she survive when she realizes that the Field Blight might be the least of her concerns?" Changed to: "How will she survive when the Field Blight might be the least of her concerns?"

That sentence went from 18 words to 15 words.

- "When ancient myths become reality by the great dragon dispatching his army to retrieve the Keystone Bone." Changed to: "Ancient myths become reality when the great dragon dispatches his army to retrieve the Keystone Bone."

I saved a single word there, but more importantly, the sentence flows a lot better with this minor tweak.

3. Transitions

If your book description fails to flow logically from one sentence to the next, it will trip up the reader. It needs a certain rhythm, where each sentence progresses smoothly into the next.

First, look at your current version of the blurb: Are there any places where the switch from one sentence to the next sounds clunky?

Try to use words like, "when", "after", "as", "before" or "with" between those sentences. These words do a particularly good job in making the blurb move along, and it's a good rule of thumb to use one of them in every third sentence or so.

- "But the world of Erisdün is nothing like Aea had imagined." Changed to: "Before long, Aea learns that the world of Erisdün is nothing like she imagined."

With this edit, I ended up adding three words, but given that the blurb is well under 300 words in total, this trade was worth it. This new sentence transitions much better than the former did.

- "How will she survive when the Field Blight might be the least of her concerns?" Changed to: "How to survive the Field Blight might be the least of her concerns."

In addition to this modification, I merged this sentence with the one that came before it. Again, it eases the transition and makes for a more pleasant read.

- "Forces, as old as time itself, make Aea's journey more perilous than ever." Changed to: "With forces as old as time itself, Aea's journey becomes more perilous than ever."

Once again, I'm accepting one additional word in the name of a more powerful transition.

- "When ancient myths become reality by the great dragon dispatching his army to retrieve the Keystone Bone".
  Changed to: "Ancient myths turn real as the great dragon dispatches his army to retrieve the Keystone Bone."

That just sounds so much better, doesn't it?

4. Variation

Variation is a good thing, especially when it comes to the length of your sentences. In that regard, it's no different from writing the novel itself.

The reader's attention will begin to drift if all your sentences are the same length. The words will turn into a blur and all start to sound the same. You need every word to pull its weight, so review your book description and ask yourself if you are varying the length of the sentences well enough.

- "Aea is an outsider. At age six the clan executed her father. Her mother and older sister left for unknown reasons, never to return." Changed to: "Aea is an outsider. At age six the clan executed her father, after which her mother and older sister disappeared, never to return."

In general I'm pretty happy with the sentence lengths throughout my blurb, but these three beginning sentences felt jarring. As covered earlier, the first sentence *has* to be short, so I kept it as-is, and instead merged the second and the third sentences.

Example, *Desolation*

Eons have turned the great dragon into legend. Tales soon become disastrously real…

Aea is an outsider. At age six the clan executed her father, after which her mother and older sister disappeared, never to return.

When her mother suddenly appears, broken by the deadly disease the Field Blight, Aea faces a desperate choice. Rescuing her sister from mortal danger involves leaving the protective forest realm and subjecting herself – and her unborn child – to the Field Blight. A race against time has begun.

Before long, Aea learns that the world of Erisdün is nothing like she imagined. How to survive the Field Blight might be the least of her concerns.

Ancient myths turn real as the great dragon dispatches his army to retrieve the Keystone Bone – the bone of a God, the only component to prevent the Arch Demon from breaking free.

With forces as old as time itself, Aea's journey becomes more perilous than ever.

Desolation is an epic fantasy.

If you like a fast-paced read with dragons and demons, then you will love *Desolation*.

Delve into the exciting adventure today.

This is the first book in the *Keystone Bone* trilogy.
(Must be read in order)

Task List

- Keep your book description below 300 words, unless you are sacrificing emotional impact in the process
- Cut repetition from your book description
- Simplify complicated sentences and reduce the overall word count in the process
- Use transitional words like "when", "after", "as", "before" and "with" between sentences. As a rule of thumb, try using one of them in about every third sentence
- Make sure your sentence length varies

PHASE 2: PERFECTION

This chapter is where you are going to turn the book description into a harmonious-sounding piece that will vibrate perfectly with your target readers.

In phase 2, you might begin to think that some of these elements could just as easily have been done in phase 1. Perhaps you are right. However, editing is a nurturing process and I have intentionally left out my instructions on completing the coming tasks until now.

As before, I have included the example blurb from *Desolation* at the end of this chapter and along the way I'm showing the changes I'm making.

Are you ready?

1. Boring middles

You know how some books tends to falter in the middle? So it is for book descriptions, and the problem is quite obvious. The reader will never get to that amazing ending, which we are going to create next, in phase 3 of the editing.

I want you to focus on the middle part of your current blurb. Ask yourself: Am I happy with it?

Since you have carefully built the book description – as laid out by this book – please don't start to think of ways in which you can add something new. The content of your blurb is in place and it should remain so. Everything has been carefully picked, and now is not the time to mess with that.

Instead, limit yourself to considering whether or not there is enough tension in the middle of your book description? If not, can you twist the existing sentences in such a way that they convey more danger?

- The example blurb sounded like this: "Before long, Aea learns that the world of Erisdün is nothing like she imagined. How to survive the Field Blight might be the least of her concerns. Ancient myths turn real as the great dragon dispatches his army to retrieve the Keystone Bone – the bone of a God, the only component to prevent the Arch Demon from breaking free. With forces as old as time itself, Aea's journey becomes more perilous than ever."
- I decided to change it to this: "Before long, Aea learns that the world of Erisdün is nothing like she imagined. Surviving the Field Blight might be the least of her concerns as the great dragon dispatches his army to retrieve the Keystone Bone. The bone of a God is the only component that prevents the Arch Demon from breaking free. Forces as old as time itself is about to be set free."

2. Sovereign words

When you developed the tag line, I mentioned Sovereign words.

This is where you trade out any boring words that are still left in your blurb with more powerful ones. Compare "scary" with "terrifying," and "harmful" with "toxic". Some words simply have more of an emotional impact than others.

In reviewing your blurb, use Appendix B for inspiration and look to make your blurb as cinematic as possible by choosing words that will lure the reader in and make them feel the great ride they are in for.

Here are the changes I made to the example blurb. I made all the Sovereign words bold:

- "Eons have turned the great dragon into legend." Changed to: "**Eons** have shrouded the **dreaded dragon** in **legend**."
- "Tales soon become disastrously real..." Changed to: "**Ancient myths** soon become **terrifying** real."
- "At age six the clan executed her father, after which her mother and older sister disappeared, never to return." Changed to: "At age six the clan executed her father and when her mother and sister disappeared, Aea's life spiraled into **chaos**."
- "When her mother suddenly appears, broken by the deadly disease the Field Blight, Aea faces a desperate choice." Changed to: "Suddenly **staggering** out of the woods, broken by the **deadly** disease the Field Blight, her mother lays a **desperate** choice on Aea."
- "Rescuing her sister from mortal danger involves leaving the protective forest realm and subjecting herself – and her unborn child – to the Field Blight." Changed to: "To leave the protective forest realm and save her sister from **mortal danger**. In a race against time, Aea puts the noose of the Field Blight around not only her own neck, but also that of her unborn child."
- "Before long, Aea learns that the world of Erisdün is

nothing like she imagined." Changed to: "Before long, Aea **discovers** that the world of Erisdün is nothing like she imagined."

- "Forces as old as time itself are about to be set free." Changed to: "**Powers** as old as time itself are about to set the world on **fire**."

3. Unnecessary words

Alright, you are getting there, but since you have modified the middle, and tweaked the text by including Sovereign words, you might have accidentally introduced a few filler words.

Make sure none of these escape you by looking for any "that" words. The words up to and including "that" can often be eliminated.

The same is true for the word "the".

These two words are often culprits that end up dragging the prose. Get rid of them if you can.

4. Read aloud

Read your description out loud and in doing so, check that you aren't tripping over any words. It needs to flow as smoothly as possible.

You might not like speaking out loud, but this is one of those situations where reading in your own head won't tell you whether or not you are hitting the right chord. A guitar player might be able to hum the melody in his own mind, but it's not until he actually plays the tune that it becomes clear whether or not the rhythm is there. Do the same thing with your blurb.

If you need to change anything to ensure that the cadence is there from beginning to end, go ahead and do so.

- "Eons have turned the great dragon into legend." Changed to: "Eons have shrouded the giant dragon in legend."

Example, *Desolation*

Eons have shrouded the giant dragon in legend. Ancient myths soon become terrifyingly real…

Aea is an outsider. At age six the clan executed her father and when her mother and sister disappeared, Aea's life spiraled into chaos.

Suddenly staggering out of the woods, broken by the deadly disease the Field Blight, her mother lays a desperate choice on Aea. To leave the protective forest realm and save her sister from mortal danger.

In a race against time, Aea puts the noose of the Field Blight around not only her own neck, but also that of her unborn child.

Before long, Aea discovers that the world of Erisdün is nothing like she imagined. Surviving the Field Blight might be the least of her concerns, as the great dragon dispatches his army to retrieve the Keystone Bone.

The bone of a God is the only component that prevents the Arch Demon from breaking free. Powers as old as time itself are about to set the world on fire.

Desolation is an epic fantasy.

If you like a fast-paced read with dragons and demons, then you will love *Desolation*.

Delve into the exciting adventure today.

This is the first book in the *Keystone Bone* trilogy.
(Must be read in order)

Task List

- Review the middle section of your blurb and make sure that it's as exciting as the beginning and the end
- Introduce Sovereign words to supercharge your book description
- Get rid of any unnecessary words – "that" and "the" – which might have sneaked their way in
- Read your blurb out aloud and make sure everything flows smoothly from beginning to end

PHASE 3: EXTRAORDINARY ENDING

A t this stage, your book description has been raised and nurtured so much that you might be on your tenth draft.

For some of you, you will already have nailed the entire book description. If that's the case, view this chapter as a sort of checklist. For others, it might be necessary to do a few more updates to ensure that the blurb ends with a bang.

With the ending, you are looking to take the reader to the highest possible peak of the mountain and leave them there, right on the edge of the cliff.

An epic cliffhanger, where the reader is dying to know what happens next, is by far the most optimal way to conclude your blurb.

At the end of the day, there is only a singe goal with the words you have now been laboring so hard over: To make the sale!

So, how do we make a cliffhanger that closes the deal? Your best option is to end with either a question or a statement.

I should add that BookBub* has done extensive A/B split testing on the use of Questions vs. Statements. They found that it made little difference. Neither one outperformed the other when it came to engagement and conversion levels. In other words, either one is a valid method.

BookBub works with all major eBook retailers and partners with thousands of the industry's leading publishers and authors to promote books.

If you choose the question approach, remember what was said back in *Step 4, Escalate Tension*. Use "how" questions, rather than "can" or "will". The latter options only lead to "yes" or "no" answers. That isn't very exciting.

"Will Frodo defeat the ultimate evil?"

Yes, of course. He is the hero, and heroes tend to save the world.

"How will Frodo defeat the ultimate evil?"

Now my curiosity is piqued. I don't know how. Let me read the book and find out.

A statement is the other way in which you can end your book description. That's exactly what I did with our example blurb, "Powers as old as time itself are about to set the world on fire."

What you see from this example is that the statement doesn't have to show the protagonist hanging on by his or her fingernails. I have certainly placed Aea's life in mortal danger, but the threat is angled at the entire world instead. Either way is just as effective.

Over to you... It's time to review your last line. Does it end on a satisfying cliffhanger, or do you need to update it?

Once you are done, glance over the last word in all of your sentences. Does each sentence end with the most impacting word? Instead of "It was chaos in Aea's life", write "Aea's life was in chaos."

'Chaos' is the word that delivers the punch, so put it at the end.

When you are happy with your cliffhanger ending, and have checked the last word in each of your sentences, please read the entire blurb out loud one last time.

All good? Then I have to say, well done. You made it!

Just look at the transformation. This is where we came from:

Example, *Desolation,* **first version**

Eons have turned the great dragon into legend. Tales soon become disastrously real...

Aea is an outsider. The clan executed her father when she was only six years old. Her mother and older sister left for unknown reasons, never to return.

When her mother suddenly turns up, broken by the deadly disease the Field Blight, Aea faces a desperate choice. Leaving the protective forest realm to save her lost sister involves subjecting herself, and her unborn child, to the Field Blight.

Aware of her sister being in mortal danger, Aea gambles everything in a race against time. But, outside the forest, the world of Erisdün is nothing like Aea had ever imagined.

How will she survive when she realizes that the Field Blight might be the least of her concerns? When ancient myths become reality by the great dragon dispatching his army to retrieve the Keystone

Bone – the bone of a God, the only component to prevent the
Arch Demon from breaking free.

Forces, as old as time itself, make Aea's journey more perilous
than ever.

Desolation is an epic fantasy.

If you like a fast-paced read with dragons and demons, then you
will love *Desolation*.

Delve into the exciting adventure today.

This is the first book in the *Keystone Bone* trilogy.
(Must be read in order)

And this is where we ended up:

Example, *Desolation*, **final version**

Eons has shrouded the giant dragon in legend. Ancient myths
soon become terrifyingly real…

Aea is an outsider. At age six the clan executed her father and
when her mother and sister disappeared, Aea's life spiraled into
chaos.

Suddenly staggering out of the woods, broken by the deadly
disease the Field Blight, her mother lays a desperate choice on
Aea. To leave the protective forest realm and save her sister from
mortal danger.

In a race against time, Aea puts the noose of the Field Blight
around not only her own neck, but also that of her unborn child.

Before long, Aea discovers that the world of Erisdün is nothing like she imagined. Surviving the Field Blight might be the least of her concerns, as the great dragon dispatches his army to retrieve the Keystone Bone.

The bone of a God is the only component that will prevent the Arch Demon from breaking free. Powers as old as time itself are about to set the world on fire.

Desolation is an epic fantasy.

If you like a fast-paced read with dragons and demons, then you will love *Desolation*.

Delve into the exciting adventure today.

This is the first book in the *Keystone Bone* trilogy.
(Must be read in order)

Wow. What a difference.

One final remark for this chapter. Make sure that the blurb is proofread over and over again. A spelling or grammatical error is going to be devastating when it comes to convincing a reader to take a chance on your book. I strongly advise that you pay a professional editor to go over it for you – several times!

Never, ever skip this part.

Task List

- Make sure that the blurb ends on a cliffhanger
- Check that the last word in each sentence is the most impacting one

- Proofread, proofread, proofread

FEEDBACK AND FORMATTING

FEEDBACK

Y ou are probably used to working with beta readers for your novels and value their input.

I would always advise you to solicit feedback when it comes to your book description, too. Having gone through all the previous chapters, your blurb is already of a high standard; however, who is to say that one of the lines isn't working? Perhaps you think it's perfect, but others won't.

It's important that those you ask are regular readers of the fantasy genre, so I suggest that you reach out to your email list and ask them for feedback.

As always, people have lots and lots of opinions, so just as when you are dealing with beta readers, you will be looking for patterns. If enough people point out the exact same issue, then you know that it's time to listen. If only a single person has an issue with a particular element, you are safe to ignore it.

You are most welcome to join our closed Facebook group, AmWritingFantasy, and post your book description there for input. Just click here: http://bit.ly/2ysFMZd and ask to join. It's a highly engaging group with lots of fantasy authors. We love to help one another.

If you do end up making any changes, make sure to go back through the three editing phases to make sure that any rewrite hasn't introduced new problems.

Task List

- Acquire feedback on your book description by either asking your email list or joining the AmWritingFantasy Facebook group
- Consult the editing phases if you used the feedback to update the blurb in order to ensure that no new errors were introduced

FORMATTING

As with any good ad, it's not enough that it sounds good: it also has to look the part.

If you have huge blocks of text without any interruption – bolding, italics and some other form of highlighting – it isn't going to be visually appealing to the reader. Most will simply click away.

Our minds are image processors, not text processors. Anything we can do not to overwhelm the readers as they browse sites like Amazon will increase the chance of a sale.

The tool at our disposal is called HTML.

It sounds scary, but it really isn't.

HTML is Hypertext Markup Language, which in its simplest form is a way of telling the computer how it should display text on the page.

When you input a book description on sites like Amazon, you will only be able to produce plain text. In KDP there are no options for bold, italics or the like. All text will appear exactly the same.

While there is a way around this through Amazon Author Central, it still isn't smooth sailing. Besides, it won't help you much on other retailer sites where you might be selling your books, too. So, you need to learn a little bit of simple and basic HTML coding.

HTML requires opening tags and closing tags.

Opening tags look like this: < >

Closing tags look like this: < / >

If you want to make a word appear in bold, you need to use the opening and closing tags in conjunction with the code for bolding text, which is the letter "b".

Let's bold the tag line from our *Desolation* example to show what the text would look like with the HTML coding attached.

The plain text reads: "Eons have shrouded the giant dragon in legend. Ancient myths soon become terrifyingly real…" Pasted into Amazon like this, it would appear as plain text.

With HTML coding it looks like this: "Eons have shrouded the giant dragon in legend. Ancient myths soon become terrifyingly real…" Pasted into Amazon, this result would read, "**Eons have shrouded the giant dragon in legend. Ancient myths soon become terrifyingly real…**"

The different codes you are interested in are:

- [insert text] for bold text
-
[insert text]</br> for line breaks
- <h1>[insert text]</h1> for headlines
- <i>[insert text]</i> for italics
- <u>[insert text]</u> for underlining text

You can also create numbered or bulleted lists:

- <ol>[insert text]</ol> for a numbered list
- <ul>[insert text]</ul> for a bulleted list
- To make lists work, you also need the <li> tag.

Here is what it looks like: "Here is a list of benefits from this book: <ul><li>[bullet 1]<li>[bullet 2]<li>[bullet 3]</ul>".

On the web page, it would read like this:

Here is a list of benefits from this book
- Bullet 1
- Bullet 2
- Bullet 3

All of these HTML codes work in exactly the same way. A start tag, together with the code, then your text, followed by an end tag, with a slash in front of the code.

Once you have written your HTML text, simply copy and paste it into the book description field at the online retailer, e.g. Amazon, site. It will now display nicely on the store front when readers find your book.

However, let's make things even simpler. Here are two real-time HTML editors that will do the entire thing for you.

The first one is: http://kindlepreneur.com/amazon-book-description-generator/

You simply paste in your book description, highlight and click the buttons to make your blurb appear the way you want. When finished, click "Generate My Code". Copy and paste the code onto Amazon and other storefronts where you are selling books. It doesn't get any easier than that.

The other tool is also free to use. It's available here: http://htmledit.squarefree.com/

This second one isn't as simple as copy and paste, but it has a split screen. At the top, you type in your HTML coded text, using what I have described above, and the lower half will then display how your description will show up on Amazon and other retailers. This is a very neat way of ensuring that you haven't made any mistakes.

Alright, a few design guidelines around formatting:

- **Tag line**: The first sentence is the attention grabber, so it should always be displayed in bold.
- **Bolding**: You can bold words throughout the description if you want, but remember that the blurb needs to be visually appealing. Don't overdo it.
- **Italics**: Italics work particularly well for the last part of your blurb. I prefer to have all the text following the cliffhanger in italics. This also serves the cliffhanger well and it's then the last sentence before the change in font.
- **Bullets or numbered lists**: If your book is non-fiction, it's a very good idea to bullet the key takeaways, telling the reader what the book will do for them in an easy, digestible manner.

I should point out that each retailer might not support the same HTML codes. I know that's a bummer, but I have limited this chapter to the basic HTML codes for the same reason. Publishers and distributors can even change what they allow at anytime. It's therefore always a good idea to consult their help pages and check the current list of allowable codes. Try to work around this limitation, rather than letting it get in your way.

Task List

- Format your book description using HTML coding to make it visually appealing to the reader

BONUS

chapters

BONUS: SERIES AND BOX-SETS

H ave you ever heard the saying, "Your best marketing tool is to write the next book."

Grouping several books together in a series, and/or a box set, and offering them at a bargain price, is a sure way to increase sales. However, the obvious question then becomes: "How do I write a book description for the second or third book in my series? And how about the box set?"

Let's tackle the first part of the question first. That one is easy.

When writing book descriptions for subsequent books in a series the method is no different from writing the blurb for the first book. As long as the book can be enjoyed as a stand-alone, just go through the steps as laid out in this book, and that's it.

If it's a requirement to read the previous book(s), start the blurb with something like, "Since the events in *Desolation*, winter has turned to spring…" or "A year has passed since the events in *Desolation*…". The rest of the process remains the same.

For box sets, writing the blurb is a slightly different matter.

Box sets must hook the reader and wheel them in, just like any other book description. It's a teaser. It almost seems natural to create a blurb that constitutes the book description of each of the books in the box set. Right?

Nobody will read through a long exposition with every plot point or entire character arcs shoved in the reader's face. Such a blurb would be glazed over. Very long blurbs are never the solution. Not even when it comes to box sets.

I have three different approaches for you. None is better than the others. It's a matter of personal preference. Here are three best-selling fantasy box sets that illustrate your options:

"Winter is coming. Such is the stern motto of House Stark, the northernmost of the fiefdoms that owe allegiance to King Robert Baratheon in far-off King's Landing. There Eddard Stark of Winterfell rules in Robert's name. There his family dwells in peace and comfort: his proud wife, Catelyn; his sons Robb, Brandon, and Rickon; his daughters Sansa and Arya; and his bastard son, Jon Snow.

Far to the north, behind the towering Wall, lie savage Wildings and worse—unnatural things relegated to myth during the centuries-long summer, but proving all too real and all too deadly in the turning of the season. Yet a more immediate threat lurks to the south, where Jon Arryn, the Hand of the King, has died under mysterious circumstances.

Now Robert is riding north to Winterfell, bringing his queen, the lovely but cold Cersei, his son, the cruel, vainglorious Prince Joffrey, and the queen's brothers Jaime and Tyrion of the powerful and wealthy House Lannister—the first a swordsman without equal, the second a dwarf whose stunted stature belies a brilliant mind.

All are heading for Winterfell and a fateful encounter that will change the course of kingdoms. Meanwhile, across the Narrow Sea, Prince Viserys, heir of the fallen House Targaryen, which once ruled all of Westeros, schemes to reclaim the throne with an army of barbarian Dothraki—whose loyalty he will purchase in the only coin left to him: his beautiful yet innocent sister, Daenerys."

"A Game of Thrones 5-Book Boxed Set" by George R.R. Martin – Amazon Best Sellers Rank: #5,639 Paid in Kindle Store

Option 1: This Game of Thrones example employs the tactic of writing a book description that sums up the series as a whole. The magic comes from your ability to include Character Introduction, Inciting Incident, Escalate Tension, Dire Straits and Call to Action, by focusing on each of these elements through the lens of the global storyline. Write a short summary of what your series is about to serve as your base. Then turn that into marketing copy by following the guidelines in this book. You can extend the word count for your box-set blurb to 400 words. The example here delivers all the main content in 241 words. On Amazon, the blurb comes with a review snippet at the top, and a call to action at the bottom. In total it still counts less than 400 words.

"Book 1: Saved by Alpha Bear

Luke was forged in the fury of a massacre. Seizing the mantle of alpha from the tyrant bear shifter responsible for the carnage, he works to rebuild his broken pack. His elders insist he find a mate to calm the animal raging inside him, but Luke doesn't believe it's possible.

Cassie has been on the run her entire life. As a special type of bear shifter, her old pack will stop at nothing to find her. The

last thing she needs is an alpha digging into the secrets of her past.

One stolen moment is all they needed, but an unexpected pregnancy binds their fates and Luke develops feelings he's never had. When another pack shows up at his doorstep in search of the one he loves, an impending battle looms.

Will Luke be able to save Cassie and win her over for good, or is it too late?

Book 2: Desired by Alpha Bear
Book 3: Loved by the Alpha Wolf
Book 4: The Broken Barrier
Book 5: A Shift in Power
Book 6: Abandoned Witch
Book 7: The Hidden Truth
Book 8: Hunting the Rogues
Book 9: A Bond of Trust
Book 10: Faith in Love"

"Shadow Claw Complete Series Box Set" by Sarah J. Stone
– Amazon Best Sellers Rank: #650 Paid in Kindle Store

Option 2: What I want to show you by including this alternative is how you can open with the first book in the series and then follow on by listing the rest of the books included in the box-set. The advantage is that you already have the book description for the first book at hand. I would add the tag line for each of the subsequent books next to, or below, the titles of each one.

"A young woman unwittingly receives the gift of immortality from a Mage. In order to survive, she must learn to trust the new men in her life who are friends, protectors, and

companions. But only one will be her lover. Dark, unique, and full of unpredictable twists, the Mageri series reveals a secret world of immortals who live and love on an epic scale. Sometimes ordinary people are destined to lead extraordinary lives.

What's included:

STERLING (Book 1) USA TODAY BESTSELLER After a brutal attack, Zoë Merrick narrowly escapes death, rescued by an ex-soldier who offers her a place to stay. But something is different about her, and she's unable to control an unexplainable energy coursing through her body. Justus De Gradi is a man who can teach her that control. He's handsome, arrogant, and not entirely human. He reveals that she is a Mage – an immortal made of light, not magic. Justus has sworn an oath to protect her life, but can he guard her from the one man who has a right to claim it? Zoë learns the price of freedom...and the value of loyalty.

TWIST (Book 2) Silver is developing her gifts as a Mage and learning how to live under new laws. She is forced to give up her old life and live in secret among the humans. There is finally hope of leading an ordinary life... Until Logan Cross walks into it. Lives are at stake. Truths are revealed. And an unexpected passion ignites.

IMPULSE (Book 3) Silver is living under the watchful eye of her Guardian and dating her mortal enemy. Neither man can protect her from a dark secret, one buried within the contents of a box. As rival factions struggle to gain control, she finds herself in the middle of a centuries-old feud that threatens to drive a wedge between her and Logan Cross, the man who intends to seduce her."

"The Mageri Series Boxed Set" by Dannika Dark
— Amazon Best Sellers Rank: #14,122 Paid in Kindle Store

Option 3: In this final option, you lead with an opening paragraph that serves as a descriptor for the entire series. If you prefer, the opening can also be boiled down to nothing but a tag line for the entire series. When listing the books that are included in the box-set, you can do as above and include an engaging short summary, or as an alternative, strip it down to the bare bones and only use the tag lines you have already developed for each of the books.

BONUS: NON-FICTION BLURBS

T
The biggest challenge in writing the blurb for a non-fiction book is to truly highlight its benefits to the reader.

Last time I checked, there were nearly 8 million eBooks available for sale on Amazon. The times when you could afford being vague in your book description are long past. Secondly, it's very likely that, whoever your target readers are, they already own several titles on the same subject matter as the one you have written. Why should they add your book to their collection?

What is important to realize is that non-fiction readers don't just buy a book, they buy *benefits*.

You're most likely serving a cluttered market, so you need to be painfully clear on not only why your book can solve the reader's problem, but also on what life will be like for the reader once they have followed your advice.

As with fiction, the blurb makes a promise to the reader. It tickles their curiosity and evokes their emotions. In the case of a non-fiction book, what you are looking to arouse in the reader is trust and hope.

You know me well enough by now to realize how much I love a step-by-step approach. So, I will now show you the parts that make up an excellent non-fiction book description, one that tells the reader that your particular book will rock their world.

The secret recipe goes like this:

1. A tag line
2. An opening
3. A list of benefits
4. An ending
5. A call to action

I will explain each of these, but first, consider skim-reading your own non-fiction book and take notes on the things that will help the reader the most. What are the desires, fears, or frustrations that your book identifies and solves?

When readers read your book description the only thought on their mind will be: "What's in it for me?"

Make sure that the answer is crystal clear to you, the author. Otherwise, you won't be able to convey the answer without leaving a shred of a doubt in the reader's mind.

Tag line

A strong non-fiction tag line does a double duty. It magnifies the *need* in the reader by appealing to emotions, and at the same time promises that help is hidden within these pages.

The tag line will take the form of one or two sentences. It basically summarizes why you wrote the book in the first place. You were looking to solve a problem and found a solution. It's as straightforward and easy as that.

Your tag line can take many forms, so here are some inspirations. As in previous chapters, I looked to the bestsellers as we know for a fact that these convert into sales.

You can ask a question that speaks directly to the reader:

"Did you know that eating oatmeal actually isn't a healthy way to start the day? That milk doesn't build bones, and eggs aren't the devil?"

"Food: What the Heck Should I Eat?" by Mark Hyman
– Amazon Best Sellers Rank: #593 Paid in Kindle Store

You can state the benefit:

"You can go after the job you want – and get it! You can take the job you have – and improve it. You can take any situation – and make it work for you!"

"How To Win Friends and Influence People" by Dale Carnegie
– Amazon Best Sellers Rank: #1,248 Paid in Kindle Store

You can use a call to attention:

"Simple ideas, lasting love."

"The 5 Love Languages" by Gary Chapman
– Amazon Best Sellers Rank: #532 Paid in Kindle Store

You can use a how-to:

"Learn how to break the worry habit – Now and forever!"

*"How to Stop Worrying and Start Living" by Dale Carnegie
– Amazon Best Sellers Rank: #21,525 Paid in Kindle Store*

Your options are plentiful. The more specific you can make the tag line, the better, and remember what we covered under formatting. This is the line you want to display in bold.

Opening

Right after the tag line, this is where you tell the reader *what* they will get from the book, and *why* they must have it.

Since the list of benefits follows right after this opening paragraph, there is no reason to start listing benefits here. Instead, use the opening as a lead-in. Introduce the reader's problem and confirm how you understand exactly what they are dealing with. This can be done by either stating how you suffered from the same issue, or by explaining the problem with words that resonate with the reader.

How to write this opening will solely depend on the type of non-fiction book and your target reader, but whatever you do, do not write it in the first person. Even if you are teaching others how to deal with a problem through your own personal story, you still need to write the blurb as if the publisher wrote it.

List of benefits

The headline for this section calls out *a list*. Bulleted lists work wonderfully well for non-fiction books.

It's a very structured and organized way of showering the reader with all the things that can be gained from reading your book. In today's busy world, someone browsing Amazon, or a similar storefront, is much more likely to read bullet points than several paragraphs of explanations.

Show exactly what the solutions are to the problem at hand. Don't make them work for it.

Having listed the benefits in bullets, see if your book offers some added value.

Perhaps you have some free bonuses that make your book even more attractive – just like the book you are reading now gives three bonus chapters, as well as a free downloadable cheat sheet (check Appendix A).

Bonuses can take many forms, but I recommend that you create something that people need to sign up to your mailing list to get a hold of. If they have enjoyed your book and appreciated your teaching, there is no reason why they wouldn't want to sign up and be in direct contact with you. The email list forms the foundation of your business, so always look for opportunities to grow it by means of adding value.

Before jumping into the next section, I want to draw your attention to the chapter on formatting. Bolding or italicizing the bonuses in the blurb only goes to show just how great your book is.

Ending

Before buying a non-fiction book, readers want to know that they can trust you. That you are someone who knows what you are talking about.

Placing such credentials just before the Call to Action is a wise choice. It can form a crucial factor when it comes to book sales.

Before you panic: Know that you don't need to be a doctor, hold an MBA, or be a billionaire in order to teach people valuable information. If you found a solution to a problem, you are definitely qualified.

How do you go about demonstrating your credibility if the book you wrote isn't on a subject in which you are professionally trained?

One option is to include quotes from people who have replicated the teaching of the book and found success similar to yours. Or you might include review snippets from your advanced readers team which highlight what the book meant to them. Or perhaps you have written several non-fiction books and one of them is a bestseller, or has received some other form of recognition? If that is the case, you might include a sentence like, "From the best-selling author of [insert book title]." (Just make sure that the topics of that bestseller are somewhat aligned with the book at hand, if you take this route.)

Call to Action

In the introduction part of this chapter, I said, "... be painfully clear on not only why your book can solve the reader's problem, but also show the reader what life will be like once they have followed your advice."

For non-fiction books, I like to say, "Click 'Download Free Sample'" as a Call to Action. Then continue to say how it will improve the reader's life. If you are reading this book in paper-back, flip to the back cover to see what I mean. Or if you are reading the electronic version, look it up on Amazon for inspiration.

BONUS: AMAZON PRODUCT PAGE

H ere is a bonus chapter on your Amazon Product Page – that's the page on which your book is displayed:

Most authors earn the majority of their income from Amazon and since it isn't solely down to the book description to convert browsers into buyers, it seemed fitting to give you some thoughts on how to optimize your product page.

The cover

"Don't judge a book by its cover." That's a statement we have all heard, but the truth of the matter is that readers *do* judge a book by its cover. When scrolling through the search list, the cover is often what makes them decide whether to click and read your carefully crafted blurb.

In fact, the cover might be *the* element that affects sales the most. It's therefore of the utmost importance to get it right.

Your cover should be aligned with what readers expect to find from a non-fiction or a fantasy book – depending on what you write. We have used bestsellers as our data source many times throughout this book and, once again, it comes in handy here.

Look through the bestsellers and note what sort of design and imagery are replicated in most of them. Take screenshots of your favorites and send them along to your cover designer. I say 'cover designer' because, unless you have formal training in graphic design and have spent time creating book covers, this is not the sort of thing you want to try out yourself. Apart from editing, spending money on a professional cover is a top priority.

Once you have a draft of the cover, share it on social media and with your email list. Ask them for feedback.

Involving your audience has two distinct benefits: 1) They become invested and excited about the upcoming release; and 2) You get some really valuable feedback from readers that will help you understand whether or not the cover portrays the genre and theme of the book.

Don't forget that the cover needs to look good and stand apart in thumbnail size, too.

Title

Title text should be clean and use large enough fonts that a reader can easily make it out, even at the small scale of a thumbnail. Make sure that the title of the book pops.

Experience grants new wisdom and there are a few things I would have done differently with Desolation (the book we have been using as an example).

So, here are some tips and tricks when it comes to titles:

Fiction titles

- Use sub-genre specific words in the title to enforce what kind of book the reader will be getting. Visit http://wordassociations.net/en (a word association generator) and type in a word that relates to your book. Perhaps you are writing about vampires: type that in. As an output you will be given associated words. Not all will be a good match, but apply common sense and make a list of the words that make you think of vampires.
- Now it's time to narrow down which one of these words will catch the most attention. Go to the Amazon search bar, select Kindle Store, and type in the words from your list one by one. Note the number of results produced – e.g. 'vampire' produces 50,000 results, 'fang' (from the association generator) produces 1,000 results, and 'twilight' (also from the association generator) produces 3,000 results. This tells me that the word 'vampire' is highly searchable compared to the other two. Go through the entire list and find a way to work the most searchable word into the title of the book. It can't be proved whether or not this is important; however, one thing is certain, and that is how Amazon has made it harder to search by categories. This fact supports keywords to be of higher importance. I will leave it with you to decide, but be aware that normal Internet shopping behavior is to go by keywords.
- The final trick is to have your cover spell out the subgenre. By putting, for example, epic fantasy, on the

cover, you can also put "epic fantasy" into the title on Amazon. It would look something like this: "Desolation (an Epic Fantasy)", which again helps to convey what kind of book this is and at the same time makes it even more searchable.

Non-fiction titles

- Open Amazon with your browser and set to incognito. You are going to do a bit of research and it's no good if the results you gather are all based on your past search history.
- Start typing in what your book is about. When I researched a title for my Twitter book, I typed in "twitter a" (replace "twitter" with the topic of your book) and the text drop-down appeared showing the most popular search terms:

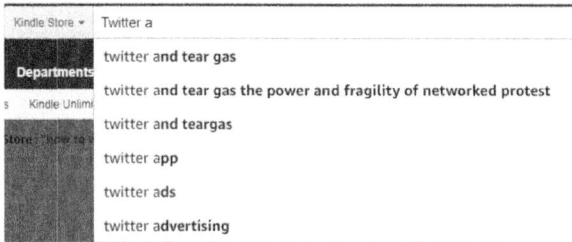

Kindle Store ▾	Twitter a
Departments	twitter and tear gas
	twitter and tear gas the power and fragility of networked protest
s Kindle Unlim	twitter and teargas
	twitter app
	twitter ads
	twitter advertising

Work your way through the alphabet, "twitter b", "twitter c" etc. and as you do, write down as many relevant keywords as you can find.

- Based on the keyword research, put together as many possible titles for your non-fiction book as you can. Then choose your three favorite ones.
- Once you have your title created, it will be easy to create a

subtitle. Use your list of keywords and make the subtitle that states the benefits to the reader.

- Your title and subtitle need to be refined until they're so appealing that they almost slap the reader in the face. As with covers, it's now time to hit up social media and your email list. Ask for feedback and guidance. Once again, the benefit is to get your audience invested; however, if your email list purely consists of fiction readers, skip asking them and instead rely on social media inputs.

Reviews

Reviews can truly be a headache for many authors. They provide social proof on your books and do form an important part of the product page.

But… how do you get reviews?

The easy answer would of course be that more sales equals more reviews, but at the same time, to get more sales you need more reviews. It's a classic chicken and egg situation.

General wisdom says that for every 100-200 sales you can expect one review and one review for every 1000 free downloads. Here are a few ideas on to how to garner more.

Autoresponder

Don't be afraid to ask your email list for reviews. Add an email to your autoresponder in which you ask for it, but realize that most people are more than willing to help when they understand *why* it's important. Many readers don't know how crucial reviews are to a high converting product page, so explain it to them. Tell them how it helps you.

Advanced Reader Team

Having an advanced reader team is a good way to acquire reviews, but do remember that if you *require* your Advanced Reader team to leave a review, then you are in breach of Amazon Terms of Service.

You can ask them to leave a review, but not demand it. Instead, explain why it's important and most will comply with your wishes.

Here's what Amazon Terms of Service say on the matter:

"You may provide free or discounted copies of your books to readers. However, you may not demand a review in exchange or attempt to influence the review. Offering anything other than a free or discounted copy of the book—including gift cards—will invalidate a review, and we'll have to remove it."

They go on to say:

"We don't allow any form of compensation for a Customer Review other than a free copy of the book provided upfront. If you offer a free advanced copy, it must be clear that you welcome all feedback, both positive and negative. If we detect that a customer was paid to write a review, we'll remove it."

And:

"Offering payment or any other incentive for a Customer Review is considered compensation. This includes giving someone money or a gift certificate to purchase your book. We consider incentives to be any type of reward that is given in return for a Customer Review, including but not limited to bonus content, entry to a contest or sweepstakes, discounts on future purchases, and other gifts."

That might all sound very restrictive, but ask anyway. You might even want to use pictures to show people how to leave reviews – and of course: don't forget to give them a direct link to the book.

If they are expected to search around for it, reviews will become much harder to come by.

Leverage the back of your book

Leave a request for reviews right after THE END.

Automated post on social media

I have an automated tweet that goes out every few days. In it, I ask people if they have read any of my books and, if so, how it would mean a great deal to me if they could leave a short Amazon review.

GoodReads

Find some groups that are relevant to your genre, but do remember to respect the group rules.

Bloggers

While this is certainly an option, it's also going to be very time consuming. Simply Google for bloggers who review books in your genre and reach out to them.

Amazon Reviewers

Some Amazon customers have set up their account to show their email address.

To do this, go to Amazon and find books similar to yours. Then go through the book's reviewers and see if any of them have their email address displayed. If they do, send them an email, introduce yourself, mention that they have previously reviewed book [insert name] and your book is very similar, so perhaps they would be interesting in reading yours for free.

Remember Amazon terms of service here, but you can say something along the lines of, "Should you voluntarily decide to review the book afterwards that would be much appreciated."

Author bio

It's unlikely that it's the bio that will make or break the buying decision of a potential reader, but for the sake of completeness, I have included a section on it here. There is no reason to leave any loose ends...

The author bio is your personal brand which also means that it shouldn't be cheesy or salesy. It shouldn't be a long curriculum vitae of all the books you have written, either. Being portrayed as a real person is by far the best alternative.

You can describe what type of books you write and why you write those sorts of works. You can mention any awards or accolades that are pertinent. Mention any fun or interesting facts about where you live, your culture, hobbies or background that readers will find interesting. Another idea could be to let people know how you got started writing, and what books you like to read. The options are plentiful, but no matter what you do, keep it short. Long author bios are dreadful.

If you need inspiration, here's mine:

Jesper Schmidt is a Danish bestselling fantasy author who also dabbles in non-fiction. He is focused on helping and inspiring others, yet the art of writing was something that lived a quiet life, in the back of his mind, for many years. It was a dormant desire and, like so many of our dreams, it was placed on a list of things to do later. It was left there. Half-forgotten. For a long time. Every summer (well, almost) he leaves for summer vacation in Finland together with his wife and two sons. There a Finnish sauna sparked his authorship. He picked writing up from that dusty corner of his mind and hasn't stopped since. For new release updates, please sign up from here: www.jesperschmidt.com/thank-you-for-reading/ (at the bottom of the page). In the process you will also get an exclusive behind-the-scenes look at the Keystone Bone trilogy.

Whether you want your author bio to be in the first or third person is entirely optimal, but the most common is to write it in the third person. That's what readers are used to.

Miscellaneous

Pricing

The price of your book will obviously also affect sales. The ultimate question becomes whether or not you are looking for discoverability (in which case you want to price low – 99¢ or free) or you are looking for revenue (in which case you might want to price high – $4,99 or above).

Series

Writing in series goes extremely well with the binging culture in the current day and age. People love to binge-watch series on Netflix, HBO etc. and have now adopted the same approach when it comes to reading. Writing in series allows you to carry readers over from one book to the next and thus increase your sales.

Other formats

Having other formats of your book is also a good marketing tactic. Make sure that any audio books and paperback books are linked to the product page, giving readers the possibility to choose at a glance.

AUTHOR'S NOTE

I hope that this book has helped you. It has been my aim to lay everything out as clearly and concisely as I can. Often step-by-step systems are good at that.

Writing a good blurb is absolutely harder than it seems. It's short-form entertainment and requires lots and lots of training to do well. Having gone through this book, you now have the required toolset, which is the starting point when building something new.

It's been my absolute pleasure to teach you what I know on writing book descriptions. I love to help other authors. I love to share. So, thank you for taking the time to read my work.

As you may have noticed, I have included a cheat sheet for you in Appendix A. It summarizes the steps from this book and lays out the different tasks associated with each one. The idea is that you download the cheat sheet, print it out, and use it as a form of checklist next time you are writing one of your amazing book descriptions.

AUTHOR'S NOTE

My wish is that you will find all the success you are hoping for.
Go forth and write some awe-inspiring words.

REVIEWS

As covered in the bonus chapter on Amazon product pages, reviews mean a great deal. That goes for Barnes & Noble, Kobo and all the others too.

I would really appreciate it if you could post a short sentence or two, sharing your honest opinion of this book. A good list of reviews encourages new readers to find me, and each one means a lot to me.

You can jump directly to the page by following this link and choose where you want to leave your review: http://books2read. com/u/31xxzM

Thank you for reading *How to Write a Fantasy Book Description*.

MORE BOOKS BY JESPER SCHMIDT

The *Keystone Bone* trilogy

Desolation, volume 1
Degradation, volume 2
Damnation, volume 3

Non-fiction

How to Write a Fantasy Book Description
Plot Development: A Method for Outlining a Novel
Plot Development Step by Step: Exercises for Planning Your Book
Story Idea

Visit: http://www.jesperschmidt.com/books/

LET'S CONNECT ONLINE

Facebook

Catch up with me on Facebook.

I usually post about my next project and future videos a couple of times a week. I would love to connect and hear more about you.

What do you enjoy in fantasy? Head on over and let me know.

http://bit.ly/28NJQXO

If you are a fantasy author yourself, I run a closed Facebook group together with Autumn Birt, my partner in crime. You are very welcome to join.

http://bit.ly/2ysFMZd

YouTube

I create new videos every single Monday and if you like fantasy settings, worldbuilding and character creation, then this is the place to be.

The focus of the channel is to inspire one another to become masters at crafting immersive fantasy.

http://bit.ly/1WIwIVC

Twitter

I'm very active on Twitter and if you follow me there I will follow you back.

I love connecting with readers, so don't be shy.

http://bit.ly/28O3ArW

COPYRIGHT

Writing a book is a project of passion, but it does require lots and lots of work.

The information shared has value and all the contents of this book are therefore copyrighted. By purchasing this book you have full rights to use all the teachings, but I do ask you not to distribute this book to anyone else. If they want to learn what you have, they are free to purchase the book as well.

It's the sales of this valuable information that allow me to continue writing books.

You cannot post excerpts or any part of this book on Internet forums, websites, social media, etc. or in any other form, or facilitate or assist in unauthorized distribution.

Thank you for purchasing this book. You are the best.

Jesper

ACKNOWLEDGMENTS

Reaching the end of a book is a special feeling. As I sit here, writing these words, I find myself gazing out the window, pausing every few sentences to take in the clouds as they float by. I always feel a bit nostalgic when it comes to acknowledgments. It matters not that I have been here several times now.

So, once again, thank you Matt Rance at ProofProfessor for your editing. These pages would have been a right mess without you.

Autumn Birt. Thank you for going above and beyond what one can expect from a business partner. You designed the cover for the book, helped with alpha reading, and even took care of the formatting when it came to the paperback. Wow. I'm blessed to be working alongside someone like yourself.

Lastly, and once again, thank you for reading my book.

Thank you all.

APPENDICES

APPENDIX A: CHEAT SHEET

Here is your cheat sheet: www.jesperschmidt.com/tasklist/

The cheat sheet summarizes the steps as laid out in this book together with the different tasks as given in each chapter.

Download the cheat sheet, print it out, and use it as a checklist next time you are writing a book description.

APPENDIX B: SOVEREIGN WORDS

A
Abuse
Admiration
Adventure
Ages
Agony
Ancient
Angel
Annoying
Anxious
Apocalypse
Appall
Armageddon
Armor
Ashen
Assault
Astonishing
Awe

B

Backlash
Beast
Beating
Beauty
Beguile
Belief
Berserk
Beware
Bewitch
Bitter
Bizarre
Black
Blade
Bland
Blaze
Blinded
Blissful
Blood
Bloodcurdling
Bloodbath
Bloody
Breath-taking
Bumbling
Burn

C
Cadaver
Captivate
Cast
Catastrophe
Cauldron
Caution
Cave
Chalice

Chaos
Charming
Cherish
Chilling
Clarity
Claw
Collapse
Conjure
Conspirator
Corpse
Craving
Crazy
Crimson
Cripple
Crisis
Crisp
Crooked
Cruelty
Crypt
Curse

D
Dancing
Danger
Daring
Dazzle
Deadly
Deafening
Death
Deeds
Deformity
Delirious
Demon
Despair

Desperate
Destiny
Destroy
Detect
Detection
Devastating
Devotion
Disappearance
Disaster
Disastrous
Discover
Draconic
Dragon
Dramatic
Dread
Dream

E
Earsplitting
Ecstatic
Eerie
Embarrass
Empire
Enchanted
Enchanting
Enchantment
Enthusiasm
Envious
Envy
Eon
Evil

F
Fable

Fabricate
Fail
Fairy
Faith
Faithful
Fallen
Fang
Feeble
Fiery
Figment
Fire
Flame
Fluffy
Forces
Forgotten
Foul
Frantic
Frenzy
Frightening
Furious
Fury

G
Galaxy
Ghost
Giant
Gigantic
Glimmer
Glittering
Gloomy
Glorious
Glow
Grab
Grief-stricken

Gritty
Grotesque
Gullible

H
Hack
Hades
Hag
Hairy
Harbinger
Hatred
Hazardous
Hazy
Heartbroken
Heroic
Hoax
Horrific
Horror
Hostile
Howls
Humming
Hurricane

I
Idyll
Illusions
Imp
Incantation
Incendiary
Incognito
Ingenious
Insidious
Inspiration
Invasion

Invisible

Irritating

J

Jade

Jaunt

Jeopardy

Joy

Joyful

Jubilant

K

Keepsake

King

Kingdom

L

Lairs

Lands

Legend

Light

Longing

Loom

Looming

Lore

Lost age

Love

Lovesick

Luck

Lunar

Lunatic

Lurk

Lurking

Lust

M

Magic
Magical
Magician
Majesty
Malevolence
Mask
Mesmerize
Mesmerizing
Miracle
Mired
Mischief
Mischievous
Miserable
Misshapen
Mistake
Monster
Mortal
Murder
Muse
Musings
Mysterious
Mystery
Mystical
Myth
Mythical

N

Nature
Navigate
Necromancer
Necromancy
Nemesis
Nightmare

Nurturing

O
Oath

Oblivion

Obscene

Odd

Omni

Oracle

Otherworldly

Outrageous

Overpower

Overwhelm

P
Painful

Pale

Panic

Paralyzed

Passion

Passionate

Pattern

Perform

Peril

Perilous

Petrify

Pitfall

Pixie

Plague

Played

Plummet

Plunder

Plunge

Poison

Poisonous
Poor
Potent
Potion
Power
Prey
Prince
Prophecy
Prophet
Protection
Prowl
Pummel
Pungent
Pursue

Q
Quail
Quake
Quash
Quaver
Queen
Quell
Quest
Question

R
Rage
Raging
Realm
Reasoning
Reckoning
Refugee
Reign
Remarkable

Repel
Repulsive
Resentful
Resonate
Reveal
Revenge
Risks
Risky
Rotten
Rough
Rule

S

Sabotage
Sage
Scale
Scar
Scare
Scarlet
Scary
Scold
Scream
Scroll
Searing
Seduction
Seeking
Seer
Serene
Shade
Shadow
Shadowy
Shaman
Shame
Shatter

Shellacking
Shimmer
Shriek
Silky
Slaughter
Slave
Slimy
Smash
Soaring
Sobbing
Soothsayer
Sorcerer
Sorcery
Sparkle
Sparkling
Spectacular
Specter
Spell
Spellbinding
Spew
Spirits
Squeaky
Staggering
Stale
Stars
Steal
Steel
Stifling
Storm
Strangle
Supernatural
Superstition
Sword
Sworn

T

Tailspin
Talisman
Targeted
Tearful
Teary-eyed
Teetering
Tenderness
Terrific
Terrifying
Terror
Threat
Thrilling
Tornadic
Toxic
Tragic
Transform
Trap
Tremors
Triumph
Triumphant
Troubled

U

Unbelievable
Unexplained
Unicorn
Unique
Unusual

V

Valiant
Valor
Vampire

Vanguard
Vanish
Vanquish
Vaporize
Venomous
Vice
Vicious
Victim
Vigor
Vital
Void
Volatile
Vortex
Vulnerable

W
Wail
Wand
Ward
Warning
Watchful
Whisk
Whispers
Wicked
Wing
Wisdom
Wish
Witch
Wizard
Worry
Worship
Wounded
Wrinkled

X

Weno

Y

Yearn

Z

Zealous

Printed in Great Britain
by Amazon